IN SEARCH OF PEACE

A Scriptural Program of Prayer and Community Discussion

Helen C. Swift, SND de N

LIGUORI
PUBLICATIONS

One Liguori Drive
Liguori, Missouri 63057
(314) 464-2500

Imprimi Potest:
John F. Dowd, C.SS.R.
Provincial, St. Louis Province
Redemptorist Fathers
Imprimatur:
Monsignor Edward J. O'Donnell
Vicar General, Archdiocese of St. Louis
ISBN 0-89243-192-X

Library of Congress Catalog Card Number: 83-81710

Cover design by Pam Hummelsheim

PEACE
founded on truth
built on justice
motivated and integrated by charity
practiced in freedom

TABLE OF CONTENTS

Dialogue on Freedom

* * * * *

THE READINGS

INTRODUCTION

An Overview

Today more and more people are feeling anxious that our world is moving toward self-destruction. Because our lives and all that we hold dear are in danger of being wiped out, there is a growing conviction that we cannot be passive in the face of such a threat. We must do something; and yet, we feel so insignificant as we grope for light to know what to do.

Perhaps you were drawn to pick up this book because you too are feeling this uneasiness. With this book you can enter into a dynamic process of individual prayer/reflection and communal sharing of insights that will open new opportunities for peacemaking.

In Search of Peace will give you an opportunity to listen to God and to bring your concerns to him. As you present your unique self to God with all your thoughts and emotions he will lead you to reflect on his word. These reflections and your response to God will prepare you to share your insights with others. Together you will grow in an awareness of your gifts and how God is calling each person to a deeper relationship with him and his world.

As you gift one another with these insights you will find that you are no longer a group of individuals but you have become a faith-sharing community. You will know something of the support and encouragement that flows out of community to each member.

The readings and the questions for reflection and discussion are meant to stimulate your thought and tap the creative spirit in each of you. As you listen reverently to each other you will share in the richness of the community. You will discover new ways of being with God, with one another, and with the world that will help reverse our plunge toward destruction.

As you move back and forth from prayer to community sharing you will experience a more vivid coming of the Kingdom into your lives. Then you will hear the call of the Prince of Peace to make your unique contribution to his Kingdom of Peace and in his grace you will find the strength and courage to respond.

The Group

While it is possible to pray the meditations and read the selections without interacting with a group, you may lose an important dimension. The richness of the program depends on sharing the results of your meditations and your insights from the readings. Each person is unique, and each brings his or her own background to the experience. Your insights bring a dimension to the group that no one else can give it. You receive from the group new ways of looking at life and of relating to God and to his world.

An ideal size group consists of 10 to 12 members. There is no need to try for a similarity of persons in the group, such as all women, all men, all married couples. Groups in which there is a range of ages, occupations, family backgrounds, and education will be richer than a homogeneous group.

The Meeting

The group will meet for two hours once a week, for twelve weeks, in a place that is conducive to prayer and sharing. The meeting time should include these elements:

1. *Song and prayer.* The song might be one the group can sing together or one that you listen to on a tape or record. The prayer might be a Psalm that fits the topic or it might be spontaneous prayer by the leader. If the group is accustomed to praying together, it might also be a short time of shared prayer.

2. *Sharing.* There are two kinds of sharing. Sharing about the meditations is sharing with the group the results of your prayer. What happened when you met God in prayer as a result of meditation? This sharing involves a faith dimension and is at heart level. You are NOT sharing ideas or discussing the thoughts presented in the meditation.

Sharing about the readings comes through the reflection questions. This is a sharing of ideas and your own experience. The goal here is a better understanding of the subject so the sharing is more intellectual and experiential. Both types of sharing are important for growth toward greater peace.

3. *Preparation.* The leader needs to be conscious of time so that sufficient time is given to preparation for the following week. The person who will be leader the following week guides the group through the preparation.

4. *Closing prayer.* It is well to close with a time of intercessory prayer. This brief time at the end of the meeting helps to build community. It gives the members of the group a sense of being supported in the concerns and burdens of daily living.

It is very important for the morale of the group that the meeting open at the scheduled time and end on time. The opening and closing prayer should be brief, leaving ample time for sharing and preparation.

The Leader

Each leader needs to be sensitive to the whole group. No one should be pressured to share, but some need the way opened for them. The leader is responsible for opening the meeting with a song and prayer that are appropriate to the subject. It is important that the atmosphere of each meeting be prayerful. Each person who speaks should be respectfully listened to, for that person is gifting the group. Differences of opinion should be viewed as enrichment, not the beginning of a debate.

Trust

Each person in the group should be aware from the very beginning that all that is said during the meetings should remain within the group. As the group meets you will find a community spirit growing. You will begin to trust one another more and count on the support and care of the group. Then confidentiality becomes easier. It is especially in the first sessions that each one needs to be very aware of fostering trust within the group.

Meditations

The program begins with five introductory meditations. The method of meditation may be new for some of you so a few suggestions are in order. Each meditation consists of a Scripture text and some thoughts that might help you begin your prayer. The thoughts are only meant for suggestions: they are *not* the prayer.

Your prayer will often involve *listening* to God's word, *reflecting* on the meaning of this message in your life, and responding in *dialogue* with God. There are times when active listening will predominate in your prayer as you open your heart to let God fill it. At other times, you will listen and then ponder the word you hear, looking at your life in the light of this message. As the program progresses, dialogue with God may become the dominant feature of your prayer. Again you listen, reflect briefly, and then carry on a dialogue with God. More will be said later about each of these ways of encountering God.

Prayer is a gift of God. We can only create the atmosphere where we are open to God's gift. You might prepare your heart to receive God by following these simple steps:

1. Find a quiet place where you can take a comfortable position. There is no one position that is right for everyone. Some people like to pray sitting, others prefer lying on their backs or prostrate. Still others find that kneeling is helpful to them. Experiment with various positions until you find one that is right for you at the time.

2. Relax physically and mentally. Let the tenseness leave your body. Let the thoughts and cares of your daily life fall away. Do not strain to clear your mind; you only become tense. Just let go of the thoughts that ordinarily fill your mind and let them slip away.

3. Recall that you are in God's presence. He is always caring for you. Exercise your faith in him to grow more conscious of his care in the past. See how he is loving you now and how he intends to give you even greater gifts in the future. Take as much time as you need to be aware of God. Until you are in contact with God no prayer can take place.

4. Read the Scripture passage and then the suggested thoughts for prayer. Read slowly, letting the words become part of you. Read aloud if possible. You will then be using two senses to take in God's message.

5. Reflect quietly on what God is saying to you. Do not be in a rush to say something. Let God have his chance to speak to your heart. Listen to him.

6. Respond to God's message from your heart. Tell God exactly how you feel about what he is saying to you. Try to be very honest with God.

The first five meditations are to help you move gradually into the program. You will need a Bible, but it is not necessary for everyone to have the same edition of the Bible. Different translations can add a richness to your sharing. However, some translations, such as the *New American Bible,* may be more helpful to you. *The Jerusalem Bible* has especially good footnotes. It is well in your group preparation of the meditations to look up the Scripture texts. Be sure everyone in the group can locate the texts.

You will need to set aside at least fifteen minutes each day to pray on one of the meditations. On the two extra days of the week you may repeat a meditation you found fruitful. The repetition does not consist in going over the meditation in the same way but, rather, returning to those points in the prayer that seemed grace-filled for you. It is a way of allowing that grace to deepen. On the other hand, you might have found one of the meditations especially difficult. You might want to try that meditation again.

Journal

Each day *after* your time of prayer, jot down in a notebook how the prayer went for you. Do not be concerned with what you will write while you are praying. You will only distract yourself and make prayer impossible. After you have finished praying you might ask yourself some of the following questions:
1. How did I feel as I read the Scripture text and thoughts for this meditation?
2. Did I feel resistance, or was I drawn to this topic?

3. Did I really find God in this prayer time?
4. What was God saying to me in this prayer?
5. How did I respond to God? enthusiastically? fearfully? lovingly? resentfully? gratefully? etc.
6. Were there any special insights in this prayer?

These are just a few suggested questions to help you understand and record your prayer. You might think of other questions that are more helpful for you.

The prayer journal will be helpful for you when you share your prayer with the group. Kept over a period of time, the journal helps you to see how God is leading you and your spiritual growth.

SESSION 1

Outline of the meeting:

1. Opening prayer and song. Psalm 139 is especially appropriate as a prayer to begin this first session. Choose a song with the theme of new beginning.

2. Take some time to introduce yourselves and share briefly your reasons for wanting to participate in this program of prayer and community formation.

3. Go over the Introduction in this book and make sure that everyone understands the process.

4. Spend some time discussing the suggestions for meditation and journal-keeping found in the Introduction.

5. PREPARE for the prayers of listening. Read the Scripture texts and suggestions for prayer which follow each text. Help one another understand the suggestions for meditation, but do not discuss the ideas at this point. You do not want to program your prayer by setting up certain expectations.

Your prayer for the coming week will consist essentially in listening to God. You have already had an experience of listening to God or you would not be starting this program with this particular group.

God speaks to us in many ways. This week you open your heart to God as he speaks to you in Scripture. Scripture is, in a special way, God's word, alive for us today as it was for the early Christians.

Listening is not a passive stance before God. It is, first of all, having the desire to hear God, to really want to become conscious of your relationship with God as it is at present.

Listening is the willingness to hear God challenging you to go beyond where you are now. As you come to listen, you are saying, by your attitude, that you are willing to take the risk of hearing something you might not like. These meditations help you to listen with attentiveness and reverence. As you meet God this week you are indicating that you are willing to respond to his message if he will show you how. You may become aware of some fears you have about responding to God. Bring these fears out in the open, admitting to God that you need his strength and courage.

Several of the meditations might need to be put in context to be more meaningful. The first meditation depicts the call of Moses. If you have the time, read the beginning of the Book of Exodus to refresh your mind about the early life of Moses. It is in this context that Moses hears the call of God.

The prophet Elijah, referred to in the second meditation, lived during a stormy period of Jewish history. The Israelites were jealous of the neighboring nations who were ruled by kings. They had begged God to give them a king too. God had granted their request, and Saul became the first king. A king was still reigning in Israel when God called the prophet Elijah.

Prophets spoke God's message to the people. Often it was a call to repentance, a message they did not want to hear. As a result prophets often had to flee and hide in deserted places to save their lives. The incident for your second meditation took place as Elijah was fleeing from Jezebel.

In the next two meditations the texts again refer to Moses as he struggles to understand and respond to God's call. The fourth meditation is probably one you might return to several times. It is so easy to pretend that we are not afraid and then rationalize our lack of response to God's call.

The fifth meditation is intended to give you the awareness that you are not alone in your response to God. Jesus responded in great freedom to the will of his Father, and he wants you to know that he is still present in the world through the power of his Spirit living within his followers.

Be sure to write in your prayer journal after each meditation as suggested in the Introduction.

6. Close with intercessory prayer.

Listening

A Call

Read Exodus 3:1-6.

As you begin this program become aware of God's call echoing through the turmoil of the world around you. Do your best to come before the Lord with the generosity of Moses, saying to him eagerly, "Here I am, Lord."

As God spoke to Moses he wants to reveal himself to us. One way God speaks to us is through the signs of the times. He reveals himself to us through the events of contemporary history. If we reflect prayerfully on our times with open hearts, we will hear God's message.

Moses hid his face, for he realized what an awesome thing it is to encounter God. God calls us to approach him, not in fear but filled with a sense of awe that we are privileged to be so intimate with the Holy One. Each time we communicate with God, we, too, are on holy ground.

Ask God to cleanse your heart of any resistance to his message so that you may hear and respond with generosity.

Personal Notes

. . . or a Whisper

Read 1 Kings 19:9-13a.

Elijah looked at the world around him and was depressed. He was alone in speaking out against the evils of Israel, and his life was threatened. He was trying to find God's will in the events of his life.

God reveals something of himself in the way he speaks to Elijah. God was not in the noise and turmoil of wind, earthquake, or fire. His presence was revealed in a "tiny whispering sound." This is the way he comes to a person who is seeking him. He comes so quietly that unless we take time to shut out the noise and distractions of our lives we can miss his whisper.

As you begin this program of prayer/reflection and community formation, find your private "cave." Resolve now to go there each day and await the coming of the Lord in a "tiny whispering sound." Respond to God from your heart.

Personal Notes

Concern

Read Exodus 3:7-10.

Our God is a caring and concerned God. He does not exist in isolated splendor, oblivious to the suffering and oppression of his people. Today, as in the time of Moses, God does hear the cries of the poor and oppressed in all parts of the world.

When we see pictures of starving children, we may be tempted to ask, "Why doesn't God *do* something?" We would like to see dramatic, spectacular solutions to world problems, but God chooses to do so only through people called to freely cooperate with him. This loving action is at the very core of Christianity as a covenant religion. He constantly invites, "Come now! I will send you!"

Be with Jesus, realizing that you live in a world full of injustice and oppression. Let yourself feel the burdens of injustice and your own inadequacy. Then hear Jesus say, "Come now! I will send you." Respond to the invitation of Jesus from your heart with great honesty.

Personal Notes

Reassurance

Read Exodus 3:11-14, 4:10.

Moses realized his own limitations. Focusing on his weaknesses, he was afraid. As long as he looked at his human limitations, he was filled with fear. Not wanting to admit his fear, he rationalized it. He made excuses for not doing what God asked of him.

There are times in life when God seems to be asking us to take a risk, to do something we have never done before. We are all naturally fearful of the unknown. It is so easy to act like Moses, to think of excuses. Some of the excuses sound so reasonable! We bring ourselves to the point of saying, "God can't really be asking me to do this!"

As you are getting into this program, are you fearful of what God might ask of you? In your prayer be with Jesus in an experience of the past when you were fearful. Let Jesus show you how he was present in that experience. Make an act of faith that Jesus is with you now in any fears you might have. Ask him to share his courage with you.

Personal Notes

Support

Read John 1:1-3,14.

In these simple words John expresses the profound truth of God becoming incarnated in Jesus. In taking on human flesh God inserted himself into our history. All of history had been moving forward to this point. Since the Incarnation, all history moves toward the future, its culmination in glory.

Jesus entered fully into our human condition. During his earthly life he was limited by time and space as we are. He preached in Galilee and Palestine in a Judaic culture. He worshiped in the Temple and went to the synagogue on the Sabbath.

The Resurrection of Jesus broke through all limitations of space and time. He is still present in the world, filling the world and human history. The presence of Jesus is active, working to bring about liberation, reconciliation, and peace. Sometimes the presence of Jesus is so mixed with the flawed activity of human beings that it is difficult to see.

Beg Jesus to reveal his presence to you. Be quiet, and let Jesus bring to your mind some event and reveal to you his presence there.

Personal Notes

Personal Notes

SESSION 2

Outline of the meeting:
1. Opening prayer and song.
2. Take a little time to share any general difficulties you had with the meditations of the past week. Did anyone have trouble finding some quiet time? Did anyone experience difficulty with the process of meditation? Any help you can give one another will improve the prayer for the following weeks.
3. SHARE what you heard when listening during the past week, giving everyone the opportunity to speak. Remember you are sharing the prayer, not ideas on the content.
4. PREPARE for the prayer of reflection during the week to come. Your prayer last week was basically listening to God in the depths of your own heart. Your whole attention was focused on God, his call, and his challenge. This week a new element is brought into your prayer. You become more active in your time with God. You are still listening to God, but you are also turning over in your mind the meaning of God's word. You are not trying to discover the precise understanding of the words as a Scripture scholar does. Rather, you examine, with a pondering heart, God's message to *you*. What is God saying to you and how does your experience relate to this message of God?

As we come to prayer we bring our unique, total selves with all our past experience. You will not be asked to remember the events of the past. Rather, in God's presence allow him to bring to your awareness past events. You may be surprised, delighted, perhaps dismayed at the events that surface. Take each event and look at it closely with God. Let the light of God's message shine on this event. How does it look to you? What does it say to you? Do you see how God was present and active in this event? Now turn back to God's message. Has it taken on new meaning for you because you see it now in terms of your own experience?

In these prayers of reflection you should have a sense of moving back and forth between God's message and your own experience. All the time, keep your mind alert and your heart open to this new encounter with God. It is through such encounters with God that we are changed and gradually take on the mind and heart of Jesus.

The prayers for the week ahead are meant to help you see more clearly how God was with you in times of peace or in your lack of peace. As you prepare these meditations together you might want to review again the suggestions for prayer given in the Introduction.

Reflection

Gift

Read 1 Chronicles 22:8-10.

In this passage God reveals himself as the giver of peace. He bestows peace and tranquillity as a gift. God gives his gifts freely, but he wants us to desire the gifts he is so ready to give.

In God's presence take a look at your past life. Allow God to show you how he has gifted you with his peace in the past. Notice the circumstances surrounding these times. Are you aware of your receptiveness to God's gift?

Now, take a few minutes to get in touch with your life as it is today. Be sensitive to any areas where you are experiencing a lack of peace. This is not an examination of conscience, trying to assess guilt or blame. Merely look at your lack of peace and realize that God wants to bestow on you his own gift of peace. Open your heart and express to God your readiness to receive his gift. Tell him how much you desire this gift.

Personal Notes

Responsibility

Read John 14:27.

Jesus gives his disciples peace as a farewell gift. He knows now that he will suffer a violent death. He wants to leave something special to his disciples, something they will cherish. In the face of the violence, turmoil, and suffering they will all suffer the next day, he leaves them peace. How could they possibly experience peace in the days ahead, days when they would miss having Jesus in the old familiar ways? How could they be at peace as they struggled to bring his message to others, as they, too, were met with hostility and violence?

As you reflect on this short passage, ask Jesus to reveal to you the meaning of his peace. What was he thinking about as he gave this precious gift to his apostles? Have you ever experienced the peace of Jesus in a time of sadness or trouble? Let Jesus show you how he was present in your life at that time.

Personal Notes

Beyond Passivity

Read Isaiah 32:15b-20 *and* Zechariah 8:16-17.

The prophets challenged the Israelites to lives of truth and justice as the basis of peace. They were to struggle to bring about peace. It sounds as though peace will be the result of their efforts. This message seems to contradict the strong conviction of the Israelites that peace is a gift of God, a gift freely given. This is the kind of paradox demanding thought and reflection that we meet so often in our relationship with God.

God is eager to give us his gifts, but he never forces his gifts on anyone. On our side, we must have receptive hearts. Our puny efforts in striving for peace prepare our hearts to receive God's gift with gratitude.

Ask God to bring to your mind how you have experienced his peace. Let God show you your part in this event and how he gifted you with peace. Thank him again for his gift.

Personal Notes

Beyond Repose

Read Proverbs 10:10 *and* John 14:27.

Jesus told his disciples that his peace would be different from the peace the world gives. Sometimes we try to find peace according to our own ideas. We try to substitute the peace of the world for the peace that Jesus wants to bring us.

What is the peace of the world? It is the false peace that we seek through the avoidance of all conflict by any possible means. The quotation from Proverbs gives one example of this false peace.

If you have ever passed over the opportunity to right a wrong because you were afraid of the consequences, you know the false peace of the world. It is the peace that comes from shielding ourselves from others' pain and anguish because we do not want to share their suffering. It is the complacency that says, "I'm satisfied the way I am; don't disturb me. Don't bother me with your hurts, your confusion and doubts, your sadness. I want to be at peace."

Ask Jesus for the courage to see through this false peace, to recognize any traces of it in your life. Open your heart to Jesus so that he may free you from any false peace and then fill your heart with his peace.

Personal Notes

Sources of Power

Read Zechariah 8:23. *Beg God to be a source of peace to others.*

Zechariah gives a delightful picture of all ethnic groups gathering around the peaceful Israelite. They cling to his garments so that he will not escape. They express their desire to share his treasure; and are very perceptive, for they know that he is at peace because God is with him.

The peaceful person exerts a quiet influence on others. We feel drawn to such a person. We sense she or he has something special, that this individual has found what we are seeking. You may recall someone you have known who revealed God's peace to you. You may have sensed the presence of God in this person. Thank God for bringing this person into your life.

Let God show you how you have been a source of his peace for others. Thank him for these opportunities and ask for the grace to be sensitive to others' need for your peaceful presence.

Personal Notes

SESSION 3

Outline of the meeting:

1. Opening prayer and song.

2. Take some time to talk about any difficulties members of the group may be having in keeping the prayer journal. You might want to review the questions given in the Introduction. Perhaps some members have other questions they have found helpful and would be willing to share with the group.

3. SHARE your prayer reflections, taking the meditations one at a time. Your prayer journal for the past week should be a help in remembering the way God touched you in prayer. Each person should feel free to share but no pressure should be put on anyone. There are some things that are too personal to share with a group. Each one needs to decide what is appropriate and beneficial for the group.

4. PREPARE for the reading (pages 71-81) to be done during the coming week by going over the questions at the end of Reading I (pages 80-81).

The readings are meant to build on your own experience and broaden your insights. They provide a common input that can be the springboard for your discussion next week.

Reading 1 is divided into four sections with a question or questions at the end of each section for your reflection. Before you begin reading, recall that you are in God's presence and ask that his Spirit be released more fully to you. The reading should be done reflectively and prayerfully. Do not try to hurry through it. Take time to stop and reflect on the passages.

Remember that you will be sharing *your* discoveries and insights with a group. This means that they can expect you to make your own thoughtful, uniquely honed contribution and be open to and expecting from them help in coming to grips with it.

Since you will complete Reading 1 in four days you have several days to pray about the additional questions at the end of the reading. The questions from the four sections of the reading are repeated there for your convenience at the next meeting.

The reading for this week contains some thoughts on peace from two perspectives. There is the scriptural foundation for looking at peace as God's gift and also as the result of our communal striving. There are also some considerations that support the thesis that world peace must be based on individual peace. This is the theme that runs through the whole program and will be developed more fully in later sessions.

5. Close with intercessory prayer. Try to include some intercessions for the poor, oppressed people of the world, for those suffering the most from injustice and lack of peace.

SESSION 4

Outline of the meeting:

1. Opening prayer and song on the theme of peace.

2. SHARE your insights on the questions (pages 80-81) that are most meaningful for the group. It is better to consider a few questions in depth rather than try to cover all the questions. You do not want to spend too much time making the selection. One way to get a consensus of the group quickly is to have each person select three questions. List the questions according to the number of times mentioned and begin with those selected most often. Be sure to leave ample time for everyone to report on their peacemaking activities (question #9).

3. Encourage people to share the difficulties they encountered in attempting to be a peacemaker, the resistance they found in other people, and any failures they may have experienced. You will want to spend some time reflecting on the successes for clues to future success. Ask yourselves why this particular effort was successful while other attempts failed. It is crucial during this sharing that each person respect the uniqueness of each member of the group. The object is not to convince others that *your* way of making peace is the *best* way. It may be best for you, but God has many ways of calling individuals. As you speak your truth to one another rejoice in the rich diversity of the group. It is in experiencing this diversity that you will each grow personally, and your sense of community will become more alive. As you learn from one another you might want to make some notes in your journal for future reference.

4. PREPARE the meditations for the following week. In your prayer during the past week you have listened to God and reflected on the way your experience has related to God's message. This week you listen, reflect, and then dialogue with Jesus. A dialogue involves attentive listening and an open expression of feelings as response to what is said by the other. In these prayers you listen to Jesus, and he listens to your honest reactions to his message.

According to Pope John's description of peace, the basic foundation is truth. The dialogues for next week help you to discover some aspects of truth in your own life. It is on your own lived experience of truth that your individual peace will be based and your action for the peace of others.

In each of the dialogues you will be encouraged to talk with Jesus about some aspect of truth in your life. In the first prayer the operative question is "What is God's idea of you?" You may need to come back to Jesus again and again with this question.

The second meditation is meant to give you a deeper sense of your own dignity. Here in the United States we have so much that fosters our human growth, and sometimes we take it for granted. We assume that everyone has the opportunity to live with decency and develop humanly.

Lest we think that we have developed our potential entirely through our own efforts the next meditation suggests some thoughts on the fidelity of God and your response. As you become more conscious of God's fidelity you are ready to look at some obstacles to your faithful response in the fourth meditation. The aim here is not so much the admission of guilt, although that may be part of your response. It is, rather, a deeper knowledge of your need for God to make you faithful and free.

The last meditation builds on the felt need of God in order to live in the truth. It is so easy to say, "I am not prejudiced," but a careful look at behavior with the help of light from the Spirit may reveal a need to change some attitudes.

5. Close with intercessory prayers, remembering the poor and oppressed of the world.

Dialogue on Truth

Meaning of Truth

Read John 18:37,38. *Beg Jesus to reveal to you what he means by truth.*

Stand with Pilate as he asks Jesus the question, "Truth! What does that mean?" Tell Jesus that unlike Pilate you really want to understand the meaning of truth as it affects your life. Obviously, it is more than merely telling the truth. Yet, telling the truth gives us a hint of the meaning of the deeper reality — being in the truth. When you tell the truth there is a matching or congruence between the thoughts in your mind and the outward expression of those thoughts. In trying to be your true self there is a movement toward congruence, the matching of all that you are with God's idea of you.

What is God's idea of you? He sees a wonderful creature made in his image. He sees a person with great dignity and worth. He sees his own life animating you. He sees a person with unique talents and qualities, a person filled with potential to become more and more like his Son.

Ask Jesus how he sees you at this moment of your life. What qualities do you find in yourself that express God's idea of you? Thank God that you are becoming your true self.

Personal Notes

Truth and Human Dignity

Read 1 John 2:24-27. *Pray for the grace of fidelity to the truth within you.*

When we contemplate how wonderfully we are made and how God cherishes each human person, we have a sense of our dignity. As human persons, certain things can be expected of us, but we need certain material things to live up to those expectations. We also need opportunities to develop mentally, spiritually, and emotionally. Review your life with Jesus, looking at all God has given you so that you could become the person he desires you to be. Look at your home, the nourishing food available to you, the time to make friends, your talents, your education, your freedom to worship — all those opportunities that have come into your life.

In view of all God's goodness, what can you say to him? As you realize more deeply that all has been God's gift to you, express your heartfelt gratitude.

Personal Notes

Truth and Community

Read Exodus 6:2-8. *Beg for the grace of a stronger fidelity to God.*

In the Old Testament God revealed himself to the people in a gradual way. He entered into a covenant with his people, a covenant of fidelity. God promised the Israelites, beginning with Abraham, that they would be his people and he would be their God. At key times during the history of the Israelites the promise of God was renewed, and the people were again called to fidelity.

Hear God saying to you, "I will take you as my own and you shall have me as your God." In this covenanted relationship, God will always be faithful to you. His love for you is unconditional. He never abandons you, even if you do not live up to your part of the covenant.

Let God now show you ways in which he has been faithful to you throughout your life. How have you responded to God's fidelity? Has your fidelity, or walking in truth, grown with the years? Share your response with Jesus.

Personal Notes

Truth and Freedom

Read John 8:31,32. *Beg for a growing knowledge of truth that you may experience inner freedom.*

What does Jesus mean when he says that the "truth shall set you free?" We need to examine, first, what the truth is to which Jesus refers. Part of that truth is the true self you have been praying about this week. Try to picture your true self. Look at all the good qualities you have, and imagine what you would be like if they were developed to their fullness.

Do you feel there are obstacles to your becoming your true self? Try to be aware of these obstacles to your truth and honestly admit them to Jesus. Tell Jesus you cannot become free by your own efforts. Beg him to work his freedom in you.

Personal Notes

Illusions

Read Ephesians 4:21-24. *Beg for the grace to be free of your illusions.*

Paul tells us that listening to Jesus, hearing his message, will change our lives. Our lives are filled with illusions which can only be dispelled by the light of God's truth. Some people have illusions about the true value of a human being. They think and act as though outward deeds or wealth or status give a person real dignity. They have difficulty recognizing God's image in the unattractive, the repulsive, the poor, and the ignorant.

If possible, go to a poor section of your city. Sit for awhile and look at the people passing on the street. Study their faces.

If you cannot go to a poor section, imagine you are in the midst of the poor and forsaken. Do you value them as God does? Do you see God's truth in them? Would you treat a poor working woman with the same respect that you would a business executive? Share your feelings with Jesus, and let him teach you his love for these people.

Personal Notes

Personal Notes

SESSION 5

Outline of the meeting:

1. Opening prayer and song on the theme of truth.

2. SHARE what you experienced in your dialogues of truth this past week. If some people encountered difficulties, you might want to review together the suggestions for making meditations as given in the Introduction. If you are not accustomed to praying this way, it will take some practice before you feel comfortable with the process. In any prayer that gave you difficulty it is well to ask yourself, "Was I aware of God's presence before moving into the prayer?"

3. PREPARE for the readings (pages 82-96) of the coming week by looking at the questions at the end of the section (pages 95-96). Be aware that you are again being called to action this week. You might want to include in your preparation some suggestions for possible action. These suggestions are only tentative. No one should feel constrained to move in a certain direction because someone else in the group is called that way. As a community be ready to affirm and support the uniqueness of each other.

4. Be sure to include in your intercessory prayer the serious concerns of the world that affect us all.

SESSION 6

Outline of the meeting:

1. Opening prayer and song on the theme of justice.

2. SHARE on the questions you have chosen for discussion (pages 95-96) as you did in Session 4. If you felt anger or resistance as you reflected on the questions this past week, share these feelings with the group. It may be necessary to admit that you are not a truth-seeker before growth in this area can take place. As you reflected on the nonviolent action of Gandhi you may have been faced with the violence of your own heart. Be honest, admit where you are, and ask help from God and from the group to grow as a truth-seeker. You, too, can help others in the group to move forward in their search for truth.

3. PREPARE for your dialogue on justice during the following week. You may find the meditations for this week difficult, for you may find your complacency being threatened. It takes courage to move in a direction which may change your life. As you begin each of the meditations be aware that Jesus shows us the way. He not only goes before us but is with us now on each step of our journey. Ask to share his courage and his vision as he calls you to share more deeply in his work of spreading the Kingdom.

Seeing yourself as oppressor may be a new experience for you, and you may feel resistance to the insight. It may help to realize that until we are fully human in the image of Jesus we share this weakness with all our sisters and brothers. To admit it and try to counteract the tendency to oppress others is already a tremendous move in the right direction.

4. Close with intercessory prayer. Let your experience of the past week and the discussion you have shared be focused in your petitions to the Father.

Dialogue on Justice

Manipulation and Dominance

Read Isaiah 10:1,2. *Beg for the grace to recognize yourself as oppressed and oppressor.*

Isaiah mentions some of the forms of social injustice which existed in his day. These injustices still exist in the world today. There are also many more subtle and sophisticated ways of manipulating and dominating people's lives. As we try to become more fully human we become aware of these external obstacles to growth. There may be laws that seem unjust. There may be social customs that stand in the way of our being our true selves. There may be circumstances that prevent us from exercising our rights. In some areas of our lives we are all oppressed. If we are honest, we must admit that in some ways we are also oppressors.

Ask Jesus to help you see how you are both oppressed and oppressor. Ask him to let you *feel* what it means to be oppressed so that you may more intensely desire justice leading to freedom. Speak to Jesus from the depths of your heart.

Personal Notes

Justice: God's Gift

Read Isaiah 45:8 *and* Romans 5:17. *Beg for the openness to receive God's gift of justice.*

To be authentic, to be your true self, is not merely an individual struggle. You cannot be your true self without becoming involved in the struggle of others to become more fully human. Briefly: Truth must move to justice.

Isaiah uses the image of dew to help us understand that justice is a free gift of God. We have to be open and receptive so that justice can take root and "spring up." This is not a passive acceptance of a gift. It implies an eager desire to be gifted and the willingness to cooperate in the growth of justice.

Paul also reminds us that justice is a gift, a gift coming through Jesus. Beg Jesus for this gift that he is so eager to give you. Ask him to show you any small shoots of justice springing up in your life. Thank Jesus for these tender shoots, and tell him how you will help these shoots to grow.

Personal Notes

Justice and Forgiveness

Read Genesis 45:1-15. *Beg for a forgiving heart.*

This is a beautiful account of forgiveness. It is the climax of the story of Joseph who had been so unjustly treated by his brothers. There was a change of heart on the part of the brothers, making their reconciliation with Joseph possible. Each time they came to Egypt Joseph became more aware of their love for their father and their concern for one another. Their hearts were open to Joseph's revelation of his true identity.

Joseph, the one who had been unjustly treated, took the first step toward reconciliation. He did not wait for his brothers to beg forgiveness. Too often the person who has been hurt waits for an apology and refuses to take that first step. Reconciliation is then made more difficult and sometimes impossible.

Injustice cannot be wiped out unless reconciliation is brought about. Is there anyone who has hurt you, who needs to receive your forgiveness? Ask Jesus to work through you to bring about reconciliation with this person. When reconciliation has taken place you will have a sense of greater inner peace and freedom.

Personal Notes

Justice and Reconciliation

Read 2 Corinthians 5:15-20. *Beg for the grace to be a "messenger of reconciliation."*

Whenever human beings are deprived of their rights there is need for reconciliation so that oppressed and oppressor may have greater freedom. In many subtle ways we are all oppressors. We can deprive others of their rights by being too aggressive or by failing to speak the truth in love. Any form of domination hinders others from acting in freedom. It puts obstacles in their way to becoming their true selves. It also prevents the oppressor from experiencing the inner freedom and peace to which he is called.

Ask Jesus to show you how you can be a "messenger of reconciliation." If you but ask, he will share his strength and courage with you so that you can be his ambassador.

Personal Notes

The Call to Action

Read Job 29:12-16. *Beg for the grace to be aware of the injustices in the world around you.*

In the Scripture passage Job answers his friend's question, "How can a man be just in God's sight?" Instead of describing a just person, Job relates how he worked for justice. By responding to the needs of those around him he was struggling against the injustice in his world.

Another way to promote justice is to work to change systems that keep people in poverty and oppression. To bring about systemic change is more difficult but much more effective.

Suppose the question of Job's friend were put to you. What works of justice could you relate? Let the message of God coming to you through this passage touch your heart. Let God show you one concrete way in which you can promote justice. Ask Jesus for the grace to put this insight into action now.

Personal Notes

SESSION 7

Outline of the meeting:

1. Opening prayer and song on the theme of justice.

2. SHARE the experience of your dialogue on justice during the past week, using your prayer journal to help you recall your insights, difficulties, resistances, graces. Since there are only five meditations for each week you have the opportunity to return to a particular meditation that has been especially fruitful for you. Your prayer journal is most useful in locating these meditations.

The repetition of a meditation can be especially grace-filled. A repetition does not mean that you repeat the meditation in the same way, going over the same reflections and responding to God as you did before. Rather, a repetition means narrowing your focus to that part of the prayer that was most grace-filled for you. You may want to concentrate your attention on a new insight that you received as you prayed. By making this insight the subject of your prayer you allow God to deepen and develop that insight.

A felt resistance in prayer can also be a moment of grace. In a repetition God may show you why you experience this resistance. Perhaps there is something that needs to be changed in your life. God can also heal you of the resistance, giving you greater freedom in your relationship with him.

3. PREPARE the readings (pages 97-111) for the coming week by spending some time considering the questions for reflection and discussion (pages 110-111). The readings are challenging you to look beyond your own lives to the injustices in the world. If we are truly Christians, we must be concerned about the poverty and oppression of so many of God's family. If your complacency is disturbed, let this discomfort move you to some action for justice.

There are only four sections of readings for this week so you will have time to repeat several meditations from the past weeks.

4. Close with intercessory prayer, including a prayer to the Spirit for light to see and courage to act.

SESSION 8

Outline of the meeting:

1. Opening prayer and song on the theme of love.

2. SHARE the readings through discussion of the questions (pages 110-111) you selected (see suggestions, Session 4). Again, the last question should be given priority. All meditations and readings thus far are aimed at action for justice. Help one another deepen your conviction that this action is essential to living the Gospel message. You may find a wide range of attitudes on this point within your group. Be open and honest with one another so that all may move forward to more committed Christian living.

3. PREPARE the meditations on love. The aim of these meditations is to allow the God of love to touch your heart. Sometimes in prayer we receive new insights, new ways of thinking and looking at things. At other times prayer results in changing our desires so that we want what God wants. In this second type of prayer God touches our wills, moving us to do something to cooperate with his will in the world. We might say that one type of prayer is mainly inspirational, while the other is primarily motivational. In the meditations for next week allow God to motivate you to struggle for justice. The readings for the following week will show how this motivation can be fostered by a loving community.

Dialogue on Charity

Love: God's Gift

Read 1 John 4:7-11. *Beg for a truly loving heart.*

John tells us that we can love God and others only because God has first loved us. God's love creates within us the capacity to love. Once we have accepted God's love he will then move us to love our neighbor as ourselves. Our love for self is the measure of the way we love others. What does it mean to love self? Basically, it means wanting to be and grow the way God wants one to be and grow. This fundamental desire implies wanting all that is truly good for self. Or one might say it means desiring all that will make a person fully human in the image of Jesus.

Loving our neighbor, then, implies wanting the neighbor to be and grow as God wills, having all that the person needs to live a fully human life. If love is authentic, it goes beyond wishful desires to action. It helps to create a human situation for the most oppressed of God's family.

Talk to Jesus about the way you have accepted God's gift of love. How have you used your capacity for love to help the oppressed and suffering members of God's family? Ask Jesus to guide you in using your gift of love wisely.

Personal Notes

Love and Motivation

Read 1 Corinthians 13:4-8. *Beg for the kind of love that motivates one to works of justice.*

The kind of love described by Paul is needed by the person who would promote justice. Helping others realize their dignity and struggling with them for justice is often a thankless task. People can be so fearful of change, of losing their hold on even a minimal security, that they resist the very things that would bring them a better life. They may react with apathy or even with hostility to efforts to raise their awareness of their oppression. They may feel angry at society but not want to take steps to improve their situation.

Are you being asked to take some action against a specific injustice? Ask Jesus to show you the love you need as motivation. He will fill your heart with this love if you ask him.

Personal Notes

Love and Support

Read 1 Corinthians 12:12-22. *Beg Jesus for the grace to be an active part of a Christian community.*

Paul describes in detail how we need one another to live a fully human life. This need for the support and cooperation of others is especially evident as we move beyond the stage of being truth-seekers to becoming justice-builders. One reason enthusiastic workers for justice burn out so quickly is that they try to work alone. Without the support and encouragement of a loving community they are overwhelmed by the immensity of the problems or become depressed at the lack of response they receive.

Ask Jesus to bring to your mind times when you have experienced the loving support of others. Then let him show you how you have been a help and encouragement to others, how you have experienced being part of a community. Thank him for these experiences.

Personal Notes

Love and Belonging

Read Acts 2:42-47. *Beg for a generous love.*

As you read Luke's account of the early Christian community try to imagine you belong to this group. Be aware of the elements that bond you to the other members of the community. Let the faith in Jesus that all share move you to beg Jesus to increase your faith.

Try to sense the support and encouragement that each person receives from the community. Being made up of weak, human individuals, the community may experience pain and tension from the disloyalty or lack of love of one or more members. The forgiving love of all is necessary to prevent alienation and keep intact the bond holding the community together.

Because there is love and mutual caring there is also a sharing of material goods so that no one is in need. How do you feel about this sharing?

Tell Jesus how you feel about this early Christian community. Beg him to help you appreciate the blessing of belonging to a loving community.

Personal Notes

Love and Openness

Read Acts 11:1-18. *Beg for the grace to keep the lines of communication open between you and others.*

This incident highlights the importance of communication in a loving community. The early Christians did not always agree. Sometimes they were angry with one another. But they loved one another so they made efforts to communicate. They tried to work out their differences, each one struggling to understand the point of view of the other.

Communication must be guided by truth and motivated by love. Sometimes it is necessary to say things the other person finds difficult to hear. If spoken with the care that makes our total communication clear, modest, trusting, and psychologically tactful, then such communication fosters growth in the community. Truth becomes more evident, and the bonds of love are strengthened so that the work for justice receives new life.

Beg Jesus for the openness and freedom to communicate with others so that together you may become more fully human.

Personal Notes

Personal Notes

SESSION 9

Outline of the meeting:

1. Opening prayer and song on the theme of love.

2. SHARE the experience of your dialogues on love during the past week. You may need to recall at this point that *what* you share is the result of your prayer. As the program progresses it is very easy to slip gradually into a habit of discussing ideas evoked by the meditations rather than the prayer itself. You will lose the richness of your sharing if you allow it to become a discussion.

3. PREPARE the readings (pages 112-129) by looking at the questions for discussion (page 129). You may find the examples of communities given in this section very different from your own experience of community. These communities were chosen because of their unique qualities. We need to realize that there are many possibilities for forming a loving community that gives support to its members in the struggle for justice. As you reflect on the readings for this week you might try to picture your group as a true Christian community.

SESSION 10

Outline of the meeting:

1. Open with a song and prayer celebrating your growing love for one another.

2. SHARE the readings through discussion, after putting the questions for reflection in order of priority. Be sure you allow sufficient time to discuss number seven (page 129). It is crucial to your growth that you make a decision about the place of action for justice and peace in your life. Some groups have developed a true community spirit through their time together, and wish to continue as a community working for justice. In other groups some members feel drawn to a particular justice action that needs support from a different community. You may want to begin considering how you are being called so you can make a firm commitment before the program is over.

3. PREPARE the meditations on freedom. These meditations will help you to make a choice. You will be asked to face some areas of unfreedom in your life. You may become aware of attitudes, prejudices, or fears that make a choice difficult for you. As you pray Jesus will be with you. He is eager to make you more free. Will you let him?

Dialogue on Freedom

From Truth to Freedom

Read John 8:31-36. *Beg Jesus for the freedom he so much desires to give you.*

In this passage Jesus did not hesitate to tell the Jews that they needed to seek the truth in order to become free. They were rejecting truth, for they refused to listen to the words of Jesus. They were enslaved by their stubborn hearts, for they were clinging to their sin. Jesus was only too ready to free them if they had only let him.

Our freedom, too, must come from Jesus. We must be willing to give up anything that enslaves us and closes our hearts to Jesus. Any sin to which we cling blocks the freedom Jesus is so willing to give us.

Ask Jesus to reveal to you the unfreedoms he sees in your life. Bring these unfreedoms to Jesus for healing.

Personal Notes

Freedom and Inner Attitudes

Read Romans 8:14-17. *Beg to be a free child of your Father.*

Paul tells us the source of our freedom. It is the Spirit of Jesus who will lead us out of our slavery into the perfect freedom of a child of the Father. Through Baptism we received the Spirit and were given the tremendous privilege of calling God our Father. Being reborn into such freedom, we must strive never again to become enslaved.

There are so many things that can encroach upon our freedom and, little by little, enslave us. We can become addicted to the values of our society — status, prestige, wealth, racism, sexism — all those inner attitudes that keep us from being free.

Ask Jesus to show you your unfreedoms and give you the courage to admit them. What can you do to become more free and help others to greater freedom?

Personal Notes

Freedom in Community

Read John 6:60-69. *Beg for the support of others in your efforts for freedom.*

The whole chapter 6 of John's Gospel is a picture of Jesus' freedom. His revelation that he is the bread of life meets with opposition and hostility from his listeners. They were all willing to eat the material bread he had given them, but when he gives them the bread of his message they rebel. A less free person might have backed off to keep the favor of the people. Jesus is so free that he continues to give his message of truth, even at the risk of losing his apostles. He leaves them free to make their own choice as to whether they will leave him or continue to be his followers.

It is Peter who speaks for the group, and they all find strength and courage in his words. They look to him, as they do so often, to lead them in their response to Jesus. As a community they remain faithful to Jesus and make a free choice.

We cannot become free alone. We need the support of a community. Beg Jesus for the grace to be part of a community growing in freedom. What can you do to help such a community grow in freedom?

Personal Notes

The Price of Freedom

Read Matthew 26:36-46. *Beg for the grace to meet the challenges of freedom.*

The agony in the garden is both a climax of Jesus' life and one of the greatest tests of his freedom. Throughout his life he had experienced rejection and hostility from the Pharisees, from the Jewish leaders, and from the very people he had come to free. He had never succumbed to fear, to resentment, to bitterness or hatred for his enemies — all emotions that would have robbed him of his freedom.

In the face of great suffering and death Jesus was not enslaved by his fears. In total freedom he could say, "Father, not my will but yours be done."

There are times when our freedom to say "Yes, Father" is severely tested. It is then, especially, that we need to pray with Jesus in the garden, begging for grace to share his freedom. Ask Jesus that you may continually grow in freedom so that you can respond to his grace in difficult times.

Personal Notes

The Struggle for Freedom

Read John 20:19-23. *Beg for the grace never to give up struggling for freedom.*

The disciples are held captive by their fear of the Jews. Jesus, risen and glorified by the Father, receives from the Father peace and total freedom. He is now free of all the limitations of his humanity. He has conquered death and is no longer subject to space and time. In the new freedom of his resurrected life he brings the gift of peace to his disciples.

The struggle for freedom is a lifelong effort. It is the sustained endeavor to be receptive to the gift of freedom the Father longs to give us through Jesus and his Spirit. We will always be, in some sense, unfree, hampered by our own humanity and the evil atmosphere of the world around us and in us. Our struggle for greater freedom always results in an increase of the peace of Jesus. At the moment of death we, too, become our free selves, and then enjoy the final peace with Jesus.

Ask Jesus for the grace to accept your death with all its attendant circumstances as your moment of greatest freedom.

Personal Notes

Personal Notes

SESSION 11

Outline of the meeting:

1. Opening prayer and song expressing your desire for freedom.

2. SHARE the experience of your dialogues on freedom, trying to be sensitive to the way members of the group have taken steps to greater freedom. Affirm any indications that some have made a commitment for justice and peace action. Let all experience the support and encouragement necessary to make the decision Jesus is asking.

3. PREPARE the readings (pages 130-143) for next week, aware that you are nearing the end of the program. It is important that you make a decision before the program ends. The readings for this week should help motivate you to that decision. Not to make a decision is to have decided against your responsibility to participate in the struggle we have been called to as Christians: to work for justice and peace. You may still experience some fear or hesitation, not knowing where the decision will lead you. Be confident that your choice for justice and peace will bring you greater peace.

4. Spend some time planning a simple closing ceremony for the next session. It is well to bring the program to a close rather than have it merely end.

SESSION 12

Outline of the meeting:

1. Open with a song of celebration.

2. SHARE your insights on the readings. Set your priorities for the discussion so as not to spend more than half of the meeting on these questions.

3. As part of your closing ceremony you will want to:

    (a) express your commitment. What difference will this pro-gram of prayer/reflection and community formation make in your life?

    (b) reflect together about the future of the group. Do you want to continue as a community, supporting one another in your work for justice? If you intend to continue as a group, make plans now for your next meeting.

    (c) PREPARE a plan for getting others involved in action for justice.

A CLOSING WORD

As I was preparing the manuscript of this book for publication, suddenly from my prayer the image of seed and flower burst into my awareness. In that instant I realized in a new way how this book came to be written.

The seed was planted during an attack of bronchitis. A passing comment in a book I was reading during my enforced inactivity began to haunt my thoughts. It was a simple thought, "Women in their middle years are the most neglected people in the Church today." I was particularly receptive to this seed being planted in my heart because I was beginning to consider a new ministry after eleven years of high school administration.

I began dreaming of a center where women could share with one another their experiences of God, their hopes and fears at this time of their lives and their vision of the years ahead. In my dreams I could see groups of women becoming revitalized and filled with a desire to spend their years of greater leisure in the service of the poor, the suffering, and the oppressed in their own neighborhoods. The concept of a center became focused on peace. It would be a place where individual women could find greater peace themselves and unite in a group to bring peace to others through works of justice.

As I began talking of my dream, I found it resonating in the hearts of other women, giving me the courage and impetus to begin taking practical steps for its implementation. It seemed logical to me that if a Peace Center were to come into existence funds were necessary. At this point, I felt confident that one of the many charitable foundations would be happy to provide for such a worthy cause. The endless hours of writing proposals, many of which went off into oblivion while others brought only a polite "No," were not wasted hours. These proposals, along with the recurring questions of friends, "What are you going to do in this Peace Center?" clarified and sharpened my expectations.

Another aspect of my life at this time became involved in the quiet development of the seed. As preparation for a new ministry, I took evening and summer courses to obtain a master's degree in theology. The final requirement for the theology degree was a comprehensive project designed to lead the student to integrate what he or she had learned. The comprehensive project is not meant to be an abstract research paper but, rather, a theological presentation of approximately thirty pages with some practical implications for the student's life. As I approached the writing of my project the question of my friends, "What are you going to do in your Peace Center?" reechoed in my ears. I felt a need to go beyond this question and answer for myself the more basic question, "What are the underlying principles for the programs you hope to offer in the Peace Center?"

The project developed into a consideration of the search for truth as the basis of one's own inner peace. As I worked at developing this relationship between truth and peace I was constantly aware of being restricted by the limitation of thirty pages, and the desire grew to expand the project into a book. I was under the illusion that this would be a simple, straightforward task — an illusion that disappeared in the frustrations and struggles of the next few years. I am indebted to some special people who were with me during these years: to my sister Margaret Roalef for proofreading the manuscript; to Frank Oppenheim, S.J., for his penetrating questions and constructive criticism; to my brother Frank, to Margaret Telscher, S.N.D., and Alma Grollig, S.N.D., for their support and helpful suggestions; to my sister Cecile Rench and many other women for their interest and encouragement.

What happened to my idea of a Peace Center for women during this time? The seed remained hidden in the dark, gathering strength from my writing. In the persevering efforts to complete the book, the hard outer coating of the seed was cracking, freeing the tender roots and shoots to begin developing. Those tender shoots looked very different from what I had originally envisioned. I see the Center no longer as a building, for it became very clear to me that the Church does not need any more buildings. The Peace Center becomes located in the hearts of both men and women as groups meet in homes, church basements, school libraries, or convent parlors, to grow in their own inner peace and unite in bringing justice and peace to others. I pray that it now becomes for you aid and support IN SEARCH OF PEACE.

This program is a movement into the world, so it does not end here. You are not the same person you were twelve weeks ago, for you have encountered God. God has spoken to your heart and you have responded. Your prayer, reading, and sharing have changed you in some ways and have changed the way you relate to the world around you.

God will continue to grace you, and you *can* make a contribution to peace. Because of you there can be more truth, justice, charity, and peace in the world. May the Prince of Peace lead you and make your struggles for justice and peace effective.

THE READINGS

Reading I
PEACE: ROOTED IN THE INDIVIDUAL

Section 1

Behold, how good it is, and how pleasant,
where brethren dwell at one!

Psalm 133:1

On Christmas Day 1977, a faithful Jew and a deeply religious Muslim met in Cairo to celebrate the Christian feast by beginning negotiations for peace. The groundwork for this meeting had been prepared just one month earlier when President Sadat of Egypt had made an astonishing and unprecedented visit to Israel. This was the first visit of an Arab leader to the Jewish state.

Through live TV interviews, the world shared in the utter amazement and joy of the Israelis. People were speechless, unable to comprehend that the unbelievable was happening. People who had given up all hope of peace with the Arab states suddenly saw a new age dawning. As one observer remarked, "The euphoria reaches such a peak that the government is worried over the letdown that must follow when it is realized that this is only the beginning step."

This event highlights, as no other in recent years, the universal desire for peace. People all over the world were united with the people of the Middle East in their yearning and passionate hope for peace. However, even in their joy, they were asking themselves, "What kind of peace?" Brought up short in our hopeful joy, we again realize that we are living in a world of conflict, hostility, alienation, and historically based prejudices. The fear that one or several of these tense situations will escalate into a nuclear war elicits various responses from individuals. Some people handle the discomfort of this awareness by refusing to admit the fear in their hearts. Others let the awareness become meshed with concepts of social sin and sinful social structures. Some wallow in guilt feelings. Another segment of society attempts to analyze the situation and find solutions to the problems. This commendable pursuit too often ends in frustration at the immensity of the problems and the feeling of powerlessness which they engender.

Today more and more Christians and other people of good will are seeing in the lack of world peace a personal call from God to work for justice. They see the need to support others in their struggle against oppression. Their response to this call can take many forms. Often it involves the attempt to raise the consciousness of others and elicit their assistance in trying to change the structures that keep people in oppression. It seems that what causes the deepest suffering and the greatest frustration for this group is the apathy they meet in those who do not share their vision. There is another and more fundamental approach to world peace. It would not only create the environment in which world peace is possible but would also provide the motivation to carry out works of justice. This approach flows from the conviction that the seeds of world peace lie buried in individual hearts. It is felt that initiative and creativity will best lead to the discovery of ways to nurture the seed: It will begin to grow in deeper personal peace. Then it will blossom in communities of peace-filled individuals concerned about justice. Finally, it will come to fruition in a peaceful world.

The awesome destructive power of nuclear weapons fills the quest for world peace with great urgency. We are driven to grasp at any method of conflict resolution that seems to offer fast results. In doing so, we fail to use the means that are effective but seem simplistic in contrast to the complexity of the problems. In one sense the answer is quite simple: World peace will begin to become a reality when there are enough people with peaceful hearts. If this seems too simple, consider for a moment the alternative. How can people who have not found inner peace themselves work in a peaceful, nonviolent way to help others find peace?

It is important at this point to emphasize that inner peace is just the beginning not the final goal of peace efforts. There are some people who feel uncomfortable with any mention of inner peace in connection with justice. They see the need of serious straining to change unjust structures and overcome oppressive conditions.

Not long ago, I had the opportunity to discuss the situation in Ireland with a woman of Irish ancestry who had spent a year in Ireland assisting in the peace movement. She was most adamant in her view that conflict and revolution are necessary to overcome injustice before there can be any talk of peace. Her fear seemed to be that a peaceful heart implies an apathetic spirit that is willing to accept oppression rather than fight for justice. Any mention of inner peace brings to her mind visions of individuals clasping and safe-guarding their own peace while being insensitive to the situation of others. I am not sure that in the short time we had together I convinced her that inner peace is just the first of many steps toward world peace.

World peace will never be attained if only the first step is taken. Isolated peaceful individuals do not, of themselves, provide the basis of world peace. However, until there are enough people who experience inner peace subsequent steps to peace lack a firm foundation. I am convinced that peace efforts have failed and are failing because they lack the essential foundation of peace-filled individuals and communities to witness to the value of peace.

For your reflection:

What do you feel are the obstacles to individual peace?

_____

Section 2

Grace and peace be yours from God our Father and from the Lord Jesus Christ!

Philippians 1:2

Like love or happiness, peace is almost impossible to define. A description of peace needs to be idealistic to motivate action. It also needs to be practical so that action is possible. Such a peace, it seems, has two dimensions: a negative quality and a positive dynamism.

It is naïve to conclude that a person who is not hostile is therefore at peace. The absence of open conflict is merely the first step to individual peace. It is frightening to realize that even this first level has not been attained by so many persons. How many people suffer conflict in their own homes in the form of constant bickering, fighting, alcoholism, or neglect! There are so many ways one person can harm another physically or psychologically. A significant number of people do not find their work situation conducive to inner peace. There they experience domination and often extreme competitiveness. Even children in school may experience open conflict in the form of unjust punishments, favoritism, excessive competition, and peer pressure. At any given time, then, the immediate task in moving toward peace may center on preventing conflict or resolving the conflict already present.

The Christian concept of peace, however, involves much more than tranquilizing individuals. It is more than holding down the level of conflict without regard for the state of affairs that is being preserved. More important are the positive aspects of peace.

From a positive viewpoint, peace is experienced as wholeness. It is a sense of being integrated, of having "it all hold together," and "being a part of everything." Peace embraces realistic expectations in regard to self and others. A peaceful person knows that we live a flawed existence so does not expect perfection from self or others. The outward sign of having achieved this integration combined with realism is a sense of joy even in the midst of pain and trouble.

The difficulties of attaining this integrity are intensified in today's society. There are so many areas of life where one feels alienated from other people, from all of nature, and even from God. Alienation is that feeling of "being out of it." It is the experience of standing alone in a group of people who are enjoying life without you. It is being oblivious to the rhythm of nature, to the changing seasons, not being touched in any way by God's creation. Even more sadly, when a person is alienated from God life has lost its meaning. To the degree that a person is healed of alienation that person becomes integrated and peaceful. This healing and sense of peace is first of all a gift of God.

To say that peace is a gift of God does not imply in any way that we should simply pray for peace and leave the rest to God. Peace, like all of human life, is immersed in the paradox of God's free giving and the necessity of our creative activity. Both sides of this paradox are evident in the scriptural concept of peace.

The Bible is the history of God's dealing with his people. There are many instances when God reveals that he is the one who gives peace. In proclaiming the covenant, the Lord tells the people if they will live in accordance with his precepts he will give them abundance of crops, security, and "establish peace in the land" (Leviticus 26:6). Later, in the time of Joshua, after the Israelites conquered and occupied the land the Lord had promised to give them, "the LORD gave them peace on every side, just as he had promised their fathers" (Joshua 21:44). Peace, then, is associated with the establishment of the covenant and also with its ongoing fulfillment.

In the New Testament, the most direct and revealing statement concerning peace as God's gift is found in the Gospel of John. It was during his last talk to his disciples before he died that Jesus left peace as his legacy to his followers. He knew the distress, the confusion, the agony of heart they would suffer during the following two days, and still he said to them, "Peace is my farewell to you, my peace is my gift to you." To help them understand that peace is more than the absence of conflict, that, paradoxically, true peace can exist in the midst of persecution, sorrow, and disappointment, Jesus added, "I do not give it to you as the world gives peace" (John 14:27). Jesus did not spell out in detail the qualities of his peace gift because he knew that for those who experience his peace no explanation is necessary. For those who reject the peace of Jesus no explanation is adequate to convey to them what it is they are missing.

For your reflection:

How have you had the experience of peace coming from God as a gift?

Section 3

**Turn from evil, and do good;
seek peace, and follow after it.**

Psalm 34:15

The other side of the paradox, that peace is the result of our striving against injustice, is also expressed many times in the Old Testament. Isaiah helps us become aware of how one's fundamental orientation toward others can either hinder or promote peace. Isaiah paints for us a picture of the kingdom of justice. In doing so he not only focuses on the delights of such a kingdom but warns of attitudes that can prevent the kingdom from becoming a reality. There is no place in the kingdom for the foolish who plan evil and "let the hungry go empty and the thirsty be without drink." The tricksters who plan crimes that "ruin the poor with lies" and deprive the needy of their rights do not belong to the kingdom either. Complacency and overconfidence are seen as obstacles to peace, for they allow the harvest of justice to fail. Justice will not grow "until the spirit from on high is poured out on us," that is, until our struggles for peace are initiated, supported, and brought to fruition by God's gift of peace. Isaiah describes the result of this joint activity for peace on the part of God and human beings. He says, "Right will dwell in the desert and justice abide in the orchard. Justice will bring about peace; right will produce calm and security. My people will live in peaceful country, in secure dwellings and quiet resting places." (See Isaiah, chapter 32.)

Zechariah, in describing a peaceful society, pictures God returning to dwell in his city, Jerusalem, and bringing about a life of security, abundance, and joy. God promised that life will be changed from the way it was at the time of the captivity, for it will be "the seedtime of peace," the time of Shalom, when the "vine shall yield its fruit, the land shall bear its crops, and the heavens shall give their dew; all these things I will have the remnant of the people possess." God revealed to the people what they must contribute to the efforts for peace: "Speak the truth to one another; let there be honesty and peace in the judgments at your gates, and let none of you plot evil against another in his heart, nor love a false oath." This union of God's gift and Israel's striving for peace will be so attractive that nations will long to become part of such a society. Zechariah describes this situation with obvious delight: "In those days ten men of every nationality, speaking different tongues, shall take hold, yes, take hold of every Jew by the edge of his garment and say, 'Let us go with you, for we have heard that God is with you.' " (See Zechariah, chapter 8.)

Unfortunately, neither Isaiah's vision nor Zechariah's dream became a reality, a fact that caused Jesus to weep at the sight of Jerusalem and lament, "If only you had known the path to peace this day; but you have completely lost it from view!" (Luke 19:42) Paul wanted to revitalize the vision of Isaiah and Zechariah when he wrote to the Romans, "The kingdom of God is not a matter of eating or drinking, but of justice, peace, and the joy that is given by the Holy Spirit. Whoever serves Christ in this way pleases God and wins the esteem of men. Let us, then, make it our aim to work for peace and to strengthen one another" (Romans 14:17-19).

In summary, we can say that peace, or *shalom,* in Scripture denotes much more than freedom from external conflict and even more than individual tranquillity in the midst of outward turmoil. It implies all those qualities that make for wholeness of life, for a fulfilled human existence. This sense of wholeness was understood by the Hebrews as flowing from the covenant relationship with God, initiated by God as gift to Israel. Fidelity to the covenant, both for the individual and for the community, was the foundation of the harmonious living that was experienced as peace. As such, *shalom* expressed the totality of the good life, a covenant relationship with God and communal life of mutual respect and love. Laws, rites, and prescriptions all particularized the demands of harmonious communal life. Looked at in this way, peace has an ethical, moral quality. The detailed Jewish prescriptions have, in our society, been replaced largely by the broader, more inclusive concepts of human rights. Whatever the terminology, it is clear that *shalom* is still desired as a goal to be worked for, with the realization that it is first of all a gift of God and will not be completely and fully attained until the creation of "new heavens and a new earth" (2 Peter 3:13).

For your reflection:

Have you concluded from your experience that peace is not only a gift but a result of human effort as well?

Section 4

For our authentic liberation, all of us need a profound conversion so that "the Kingdom of justice, love, and peace," might come to us.

Medellin Documents

From what has been said thus far, it is evident that peace is more than an intellectual concept. It touches us in every aspect of our living, in all our relationships with God and with others. It is a gift, and it entails earnest striving; it is desired, worked for, and partially attainable in the present; but its ultimate fulfillment must wait for the new age. It is a universal hope in that it is present in the hearts of all; but it is an individual hope, too, in that it is colored, shaped, and nuanced by one's culture and society. In thinking, praying, and working to bring about peace, it is not enough to count on the innate desire for peace in each one as a basis for a dialogue full of trust and understanding. Because of differences in culture, and often polar international positions of self-interest, we must begin with the assumption that peace does not mean the same thing to everyone. People who are especially committed to striving for peace tend to appreciate the solidarity of the human family and, because of this orientation, may underestimate the societal differences and the socioeconomic tensions which influence the understanding of peace.

In general, people of First World countries should make a conscious effort to see peace from the viewpoint of the Third World. The task has been made easier by the Latin American bishops, who have made impressive endeavors to articulate the meaning of peace in their culture. They worked through their understanding of peace for contemporary Latin America at the Second General Conference of Latin American Bishops held in late summer of 1968 in Medellin, Colombia.

In their view, peace depends upon three conditions: (1) as a work of justice it presupposes a society which recognizes and supports the dignity of every person; (2) as a permanent task it requires a community to constantly transform and renew both individuals and the structures of society; and (3) as a fruit of love it is an expression of human solidarity.

After dealing with local tensions which threaten the peace in Latin America, the bishops address themselves directly to the economic enslavement of their countries, as suppliers of raw materials to the industrialized nations. The terms of exchange guarantee that the poor countries will become increasingly poorer, while the industrialized countries enrich themselves through low wages and by draining off dividends and profits without investing them in the developing region. Probably even more devastating in its impact is the fact that, in the process, technicians and skilled personnel desperately needed in Latin America are lured to countries where they will find better living conditions.

Another description of peace that incorporates all the elements essential to both individual and world peace is that of Pope John found in *Peace on Earth.* Written in 1963, the encyclical has been recognized by Christians and non-Christians alike as a viable platform for peace. The document presents broad guidelines and principles which, if accepted and implemented by the nations of the world, would transform society. In the closing paragraphs Pope John sums up his prescription for peace: It must be "founded on truth, built according to justice, vivified and integrated by charity, and put into practice in freedom."

From even a superficial examination of Pope John's statement, several things become immediately apparent: (1) "Peace," to his way of thinking, is very broad and encompasses all of life. He finds in it a modern expression of the Hebrew *shalom* in that peace implies all the good things that make for harmonious, happy living in community. (2) For Pope John, world peace starts with the individual. His description of peace, therefore, applies equally to individual and to world peace. (3) Pope John's summary of peace gives prominence to its foundation in truth and its integration in charity. He evidently feels that, unless deeply rooted in truth, works of justice, even those motivated by charity, will be misguided and result in unfreedom and false peace. This inner search for truth may well be the most demanding, the most challenging undertaking of the peace effort. If carried out with courage, the search for truth not only provides the foundation on which justice can be established as the next step toward peace but brings the individual in touch with God, the Peace-giver.

For your reflection:

How do you see yourself being a peacemaker during the coming week?

Questions for Reflection and Discussion

1. Do you sense a universal longing for peace? How do you see this desire being expressed?
2. What do you feel are the obstacles to individual peace?
3. Would you count on an individual who does not have inner peace acting in a peaceful, nonviolent way toward others?
4. Has it been your experience that peace is more than the absence of conflict?
5. Have you had the experience of peace coming from God as a gift?
6. Have you found that peace can exist in the midst of sorrow, disappointment, or persecution?

7. Have you concluded from your experience that peace is not only a gift but a result of human effort as well?
8. Do you believe that the three conditions for peace enunciated by the Latin American bishops at the Medellin Conference are applicable to the United States? If so, elaborate on the U.S. situation as you see it.
9. How do you see yourself being a peacemaker during the coming week?

Reading II
PEACE: FOUNDED ON TRUTH

Section 1

Anyone committed to the truth hears my voice.

John 18:37

Standing before Pilate, Jesus explained his mission in the words: "The reason I was born, the reason why I came into the world, is to testify to the truth" (John 18:37). Pilate cynically retorted, "Truth! What does that mean?" (John 18:38) Without walking away, as Pilate did, we too can respectfully ask, "What does truth mean?" More specifically, "What does it mean for truth to be the foundation of peace?"

If we begin our reflections on truth by turning to the Old Testament, we discover its relationship to God. God is not only a God of truth but he is said to abound in fidelity or truthfulness (Psalm 86:15). From the earliest times, God instructed the Israelites to trust in and depend on his truth and the fidelity with which he would carry out his promises. The Israelites, in turn, were constantly challenged by God to share in his truth and thus to respond to him in fidelity. It is from this bond of mutual fidelity that the people saw the blessings of God descending on them.

Solomon expressed this belief when God appeared to him in a dream and told him, "Ask something of me and I will give it to you." Before making his request Solomon replied, "You have shown great favor to your servant, my father David, because he behaved faithfully toward you, with justice and an upright heart" (1 Kings 3:5,6). It is interesting to note that an alternate translation reads "he walked before you in truth," making it clear that truth touches all of life and should not be thought of in abstract terms.

"Walking in truth" is a constantly recurring theme throughout the Old Testament as the Israelites are called over and over again to be faithful to the covenant of Sinai. To "walk in the truth" meant to live a life of fidelity to God and to remember that they were God's Chosen People. There are thirty references in the Psalms alone which touch upon this relationship of truth between God and his people. The whole history of the Israelites witnesses to the struggles, the failures, and the successes of the Chosen People to maintain and strengthen this bond of fidelity to God.

In the New Testament, the writings of John are especially fruitful in opening up the meaning of truth for us. Jesus is heard telling his followers, "If you live according to my teaching, you are truly my disciples; then you will know the truth, and the truth will set you free" (John 8:31,32).

What we need to keep in mind at this point is that truth is much more than an agreement between one's words and thoughts, as expressed in the common phrase "to tell the truth." This is certainly one aspect of the broad area of truth, but it is not the whole picture. Thomas Merton grappled with the question of truth. In his reflection on another passage from John, "he who acts in truth comes into the light" (John 3:21), he concluded that truth involves more than the congruence between one's words and one's thoughts. Rather, the truth exists when there is harmony between a person's attitudes, thoughts, words, and all that is implied in being a fully human person. When there is a harmony or congruence between the reality of an individual and that person's potential for a fully human life, then one may say that this individual lives in the truth.

For your reflection:

Consider carefully the scriptural meaning of truth. How have you experienced God's truth in your life?

Section 2

**When he comes, however,
being the Spirit of truth
he will guide you to all truth.**

John 16:13

To better understand this search for truth, it helps to probe the lives of individuals who spent their lives searching for truth and recounted their experience for the benefit of others. This aspect of Gandhi's life is perhaps more relevant for present-day Americans than his nonviolent political leadership.

Throughout his life the driving force of everything that Gandhi did was his desire to see God face-to-face. He wrote that all his speaking, writing, and political activity were directed to this goal. In reading his autobiography, it becomes evident that what Gandhi meant by seeing God face-to-face was a progressively more intense awareness of the presence of God in the daily events of human existence. Gandhi was not looking for some mystical experience of God in his own personal prayer but, rather, an awareness of God in the faces of the suffering and the oppressed. His religion and his political activity were not two realities in his life but two aspects of his total commitment to his search for God.

In his search for truth Gandhi was willing to learn from all kinds of people, listening to them attentively and sifting their words for the truth. He realized that he was not in possession of the total truth. He was willing to change when he was shown to be wrong. This was the kind of humility he saw as the prerequisite for growing in truth.

Erik Erikson has made a careful analysis of Gandhi's search for truth. In his book, *Gandhi's Truth,* Erikson refers to Gandhi as a "religious actualist." Erikson distinguishes two ways of approaching truth or reality: (1) the reality that can be *demonstrated* to be correct and (2) the reality "which *feels effectively true* in action." It becomes evident in reading his autobiography that Gandhi's wholehearted devotion to a search for truth was a commitment to respond to the inner voice calling him to act in a certain way in a particular situation. He did not reason logically, step by step, to the conclusion that he should act in a certain way. Through prayer, fasting, and reflection *in* the situation itself, he knew with an intuitive insight how he must proceed.

Gandhi's personal search for truth led to *satyagraha* (truth-force) in political life. He tells us himself that the principle came into being before the name for it was invented. Gandhi first used the term "passive resistance" to describe the nature of the Indian movement for "home rule" under the British and for freedom from unjust and oppressive laws. He soon realized that this term was subject to misunderstanding by Europeans and that it implied attitudes of hatred and weakness that were foreign to his ideal.

Truth-force implies the courage to suffer, with no violence in one's heart, for the truth as one sees it and the willingness to be open to truth manifested even in those causing the suffering. In political action, *satyagraha* is used not to obtain power for one's self or one's cause but to bring both oppressed and oppressor to a better grasp of the truth. Merton describes *satyagraha* in Gandhi's life as:

> . . . simply to follow conscience without regard for the consequences to himself, in the belief that this was demanded of him by God and that the results would remain hidden as God's secret. But in the end the truth would manifest itself.

> To separate religion and politics was in Gandhi's eyes "madness" because his politics rested on a thoroughly religious interpretation of reality, of life and of man's place in the world. Political action was not a means to acquire security and strength for one's self and one's party but a means of witnessing to the truth and reality of the cosmic structure by making one's proper contribution to the order willed by God. One could thus preserve one's integrity and peace, being detached from results (which are in the hands of God) and being free from the inner violence that comes from division and untruth. Gandhi emphasized the importance of the indi-

vidual person entering political action with a fully awakened and operative spiritual power in himself, the power of *satyagraha*, non-violent dedication to truth, a religious and spiritual force, a wisdom born of fasting and prayer. (Thomas Merton, *On Peace*)

It was Gandhi's gift that he not only could live and express these ideals himself but could also inspire many others to cooperate in this type of political action. The political history of India during Gandhi's lifetime (the first half of the twentieth century) contains impressive examples of the effectiveness of his *satyagraha*. We realize that "truth-force" was not an illusive, idealistic slogan when we trace certain practical steps in any of Gandhi's campaigns. There was always an investigation of the facts of the situation, followed by a sincere attempt to communicate and arbitrate. *Satyagraha* was a last resort in a situation of widespread injustice for which there did not seem to be any other solution. The situation had to be serious enough to merit a commitment to unlimited self-suffering on the part of those seeking justice. The participants had to be convinced that they were on the side of truth and be committed to nonviolent action. The plan of action was announced publicly, giving an ultimatum but leaving the way open to future arbitration. Gandhi was insistent that noncooperation in the form of strikes, boycotts, or civil disobedience be kept to the minimum necessary to attain a goal limited in terms of a particular issue. Gandhi demanded of the participants a willingness to enlighten the resisters and to be enlightened by them so that greater truth would emerge as a result of the encounter. Even in his use of fasting as a means to attain a political goal, Gandhi insisted that one should not fast *against* those regarded as enemies nor as a means of coercion and should be willing to give up the fast if convinced of any error in his position.

Gandhi's death bore witness to his lifelong devotion to nonviolence. He realized that his life was in danger, and prayed that he would be given the grace to die, even at the hand of an assassin, with no violence or hatred in his heart. In his tribute to Gandhi, Thomas Merton wrote:

Gandhi was dedicated to peace, and though he was engaged in a bitter struggle for national liberation, he achieved this by a peaceful means. He believed in serving the truth by non-violence, and his non-violence was effective in so far as it began first within himself. (Thomas Merton, *On Peace*)

Among other examples of those who searched for truth we find Martin Luther King, Jr. His search for truth paralleled in many ways that of Gandhi. At an early age he became determined to better the condition of his people. He was convinced that he should work against segregation and discrimination toward blacks in so many areas of life. As King searched for a way to change political structures he became acquainted with the life of Gandhi. He was deeply influenced by Gandhi's example of nonviolent action to obtain justice and resolved to follow his example. He, too, paid the price of his leadership and influence by his death at the hand of an assassin.

For your reflection:

Do you believe that "truth-force" as used by Gandhi would be effective in unjust situations today? Why or why not?

Section 3

The way of truth I have chosen.

Psalm 119:30

Merton himself wrote many articles on nonviolence and spoke out strongly against the apathy and ignorance that can lead to destruction. Merton, as Gandhi, saw the close relationship between nonviolence and truth. He believed that the goal of nonviolence is not power but truth. Nonviolence is not aimed at getting political results but at manifesting fundamental truth.

Struggling for justice and peace from this stance involves a tremendous challenge. One is aware of the unjust situation but resists the inclination to use force or coercion to change the condition. It goes even beyond the rejection of inflicting physical or bodily harm on the oppressor, and takes care to avoid even humiliating him or causing him any psychological harm. It is a recognition of the truth that even the oppressor, the one causing harm to others by unjust oppression, is also a person with human dignity and worth. The desire is to so respond to this unjust condition that the oppressor, too, recognizes the truth and changes. It includes the readiness to admit that one does not have complete truth and the willingness to change in the presence of greater truth. Peace is served when both sides arrive at a clearer perception of the truth and act according to the new insight. No one who has attempted this approach to injustice will claim it is an easy method, but it is becoming more and more evident to many that meeting injustice with violence and hatred results in the oppressed becoming, in turn, oppressors because their hearts are filled with a spirit of violence and retaliation.

Much of what Thomas Merton wrote about peace was written in the context of the Vietnam War and, earlier, in the context of the Cold War with Russia. In a time of great confusion and controversy, of tension and increasing fear, he did not believe in choosing sides. Rather, he saw it as the Christian's responsibility to seek God, the truth, and the good of the whole human family. Merton stresses the necessity of each individual's searching for the truth about himself and his situation, since only with this as the basis of his moral choices could he save the world from destruction. It depends on each person to help create the climate which makes peace not only possible but a reality.

In a powerful passage Merton brings us face to face with the alternatives to peace in an age of nuclear weapons:

There is no need to insist that in a world where another Hitler is not only possible but likely the mere existence of such weapons constitutes the most tragic and serious problem that the human race has ever had to contend with. Are the masses of the world, including you and me, to resign ourselves to our fate and march on to global suicide without resistance, simply bowing our heads and obeying our leaders as showing us the "will of God"? On the contrary, this brings us face to face with the greatest and most agonizing moral issue of our time. This issue is not merely the possible destruction of the human race by a sudden explosion of violence. It is something more subtle — more demonic. If we continue to be morally passive and irresponsible, if we yield to the theoretically irresistible determinism and to vague "historic forces" without striving to resist and to control them, if we let these forces drive us to demonic activism in the realm of politics and technology, we face the *moral responsibility of global suicide.* Much more than that, we are going to find ourselves gradually moving into a situation in which we are practically compelled by the "logic of circumstances" deliberately *to choose the course that leads to destruction.* The free choice of global suicide made in desperation by the world's leaders and ratified by the consent of their citizens would be a moral evil second only to the Crucifixion. (Thomas Merton, *On Peace*. Italics, Merton's)

In reading this passage, some might try to avoid the seriousness of their obligation by saying that Merton was overreacting, that looking at the world situation from a cloistered monastery tended to give him a dark picture of the outside world. However, the contrary may well be a truer appraisal. By the very fact that he was, in a sense, withdrawn from the world situation and a scholarly, reflective, contemplative person, Merton could see the world situation in a clearer perspective. He felt called by his very vocation as a contemplative to reflect on ways of bringing about unity and peace. He believed that by considering the world from a different vantage point he could make his unique contribution to peace.

For your reflection:

Merton wrote forcefully of the danger of moving to a position "in which we are practically compelled by the 'logic of circumstances' deliberately *to choose the course that leads to destruction.*" What evidence do you see that we are moving in this direction today?

Section 4

It is the Spirit who testifies to this, and the Spirit is truth.

1 John 5:6

Not so well-known, but another searcher for truth from whom we can learn much, is Simone Weil. She not only could verbalize her own inner longings but was skilled in challenging her friends to greater integrity. In her copious writings and in the witness of her life Simone has left us clear testimony to her intense, persevering love of truth.

Her school days were spent in Paris during the upheaval of World War ı. Even then she was known as a searcher for truth. She challenged her friends to discussions on controversial subjects so that in the exchange they could all come to a deeper understanding of truth. She believed there should be no discrepancy between one's beliefs and one's way of life. She was so adamant in this conviction that she often seemed harsh and rude to those who compromised the truth or seemed insincere. Still she could be understanding of those who, through ignorance or idealism, were too ready to accept the ideas of others.

Simone's search for truth was not a sterile activity but flowed into the action that kept her life in congruence with her growth in intellectual truth. At first she believed that the lot of the working class could only be improved by a revolution, but later became convinced that changes in the use of technology were needed to avoid the dehumanizing effect of factory work. In order to discover what those changes might involve and also to be in solidarity with the oppressed, she left her teaching position in 1934 and spent the following year working in a factory.

Simone's wage was so small that she was forced to live in an unheated room, eating only the poorest food. In spite of her poor living conditions, she suffered most from the dehumanizing effect of working all day on a conveyor belt. She tried to visualize ways of changing the work pattern so that workers were no longer cogs in the system. She saw these efforts as freeing the workers to realize more fully their human potential. In all this she was seeking greater truth for herself and her fellow workers.

Simone's health, while never good, deteriorated markedly after the beginning of World War II. At this time in her life she spent many hours reading the history of religions and studying Catholicism. She felt drawn to Catholicism and consulted many learned priests in Europe and, later, in America, trying to resolve the intellectual problems which kept her from being baptized. Strange as it may seem, it was her profound love for truth that was her stumbling block. She firmly believed that she would be abdicating her freedom to seek the truth if she joined the Church. In her *Spiritual Autobiography* she links her convictions and her hopes in regard to truth with her trust in Christ. She says, "For it seems to me certain, and I still think so today, that one can never wrestle enough with God if one does so out of pure regard for the truth. Christ likes us to prefer truth to him because, before being Christ, he is truth. If one turns aside from him to go toward the truth one will not go far before falling into his arms."

We find in Simone not only a determination to find abstract truth, nor a desire to become more truly human herself, but an incessant call to be in solidarity with all those who were suffering oppression, poverty, and hunger. She wanted to find the truth in the experience itself. She could not bear the thought of being comfortable and well-fed while others lacked the necessities of life. Her desire was to share in the misfortune of others so that, understanding their plight from her own experience, she could find some solution for the injustice. This was the motivation behind the year she spent working in a factory and her months in the harvest fields of France. This was also the motivation that led her to starve with the starving people of France during World War II. She shared not only in their hunger but also in their deaths, for she died of starvation and tuberculosis on August 24, 1943.

For your reflection:

Reflect on your own work experience. Are you aware of any

dehumanizing aspects of your work, now or in the past? How have you responded to these injustices?

Section 5

**You will know the truth,
and the truth will set you free.**

John 8:32

A thoughtful reading of the lives of these individuals would yield a deeper understanding of the importance of integrity in their lives than can be given in these brief accounts. Although very different in background, heritage, education, cultural advantages, and even in faith, they each sought throughout life for the truth of their existence. They were never satisfied, never settled in a static complacency. They suffered as they followed the path of truth; and still one can find in their writings a sense of peace in the realization that they, in being truly *in* the social situation, affected by and reacting to it, were striving for all they were meant to be. Each one saw this striving in terms of a relationship with God, although their concepts of God were, in a sense, unique. Out of the search of each there came some type of work for others, some attempt to right the injustices of the world and to help provide the atmosphere where people could be free in exercising their rights.

In their very uniqueness, these persons give us a model in our search for truth. Each person is unique, so there is no one path to follow. There are no rigid rules that will guarantee the success of the search. There are only guidelines which we must incorporate into the very stuff of our lives, giving them substance and form in our own unique personalities.

By recalling that the particular aspect of truth pertinent to our discussion is the congruence existing between the life of an individual and the concept of a fully human life, we realize that the guidelines needed should lead us to greater humanness. They should answer the question, "What does it mean to be fully human?"

This question has been answered with developing precision in recent documents of the Church. Pope John based his writings on peace on the fundamental principle that every human being is a person with intelligence and free will. From this personhood are seen to flow rights and duties that are universal, inviolable, and inalienable.

In *Peace on Earth,* Pope John deliberately borrowed from the "Universal Declaration of Human Rights," adopted by the United Nations General Assembly in 1948. He presents and elaborates many of the same rights from a Christian viewpoint. He does not take it for granted that all people are familiar with their human rights but spells them out for us beginning with the right to life, bodily integrity, and everything one needs for the development of life. Among these necessities are food, clothing, shelter, medical care, and social services. A person has a right to these necessities and should not be deprived of them through circumstances that are no fault of his own, such as sickness, inability to work, widowhood, or old age.

These rights deal with one's physical needs; and one whose concerns are limited to this level is totally immersed in a struggle for survival, security, and physical pleasure. He is self-centered, with few skills, limited to coping with his physical needs, and his actions are reactive rather than creative. Such an individual tends to deal with others in a manipulative way in order to fulfill self-centered desires, and cannot cope with the complexity of a truly social life.

But how could Pope John hope that a heightened awareness of these basic human rights would possibly contribute to the inner peace of such individuals? His hope was that by becoming aware of possessing these rights merely by birth as persons, not due to the generosity of government, they would grow in self-dignity and appreciation of their self-worth.

Fortunately, in the First and Second Worlds many people have had the opportunity to move beyond this first stage of development. Why is it so important, then, for these people to reflect on their basic rights? It seems that this is one way of identifying with the poor and the oppressed who, as human beings, have these same rights. In this regard, there is no difference between any individual in affluent countries and the poorest person of the most poverty-stricken country. Both have *exactly* the same human rights; but until the need for food, shelter, health care, and security are met the human fulfillment of those trapped in poverty will be limited to this level. By coming to grips with this truth the affluent person can become free of some of the prejudices against the poor, free from viewing the poor as lazy, apathetic, vulgar, or immoral.

But mere existence and physical development are not to be identified with a "fully human life," and Pope John in *Peace on Earth* goes on to assert the universal right of all persons to respect, to a good reputation, to freedom to search for truth, to freedom in expressing and communicating opinions. All have the right to share in the benefits of culture through a basic education, a professional or technical training in accord with their gifts and talents. Spiritually, each person has the right to worship God and to profess that belief privately and publicly. It is interesting to note that Pope John, in specifying the right to freely choose a state of life, mentions specifically that in family life the man and woman have equal rights and duties.

Turning to the economic sphere, Pope John mentions first the right to free initiative in the economic field and the right to work. The right to work includes the right to working conditions that are not injurious to health, to adequate safety measures, and to conditions where morals are safeguarded. Linked closely to the right to work is the right to a just wage in proportion to available resources.

A cursory reading of these rights as guidelines may lead to intellectual assent and nothing more. What is needed is serious reflection on the truths embodied in these rights and application to one's life. Once a heightened awareness of these rights becomes habitual, some significant consequences may follow:

1. An analysis of one's own existential situation may reveal, even in highly favorable conditions, rights that are not being respected. And this, together with observation of the lives of others, may lead one to realize that, alone, each individual is impotent in claiming his or her missing rights. For example, a man who works

full time but is not paid a wage that permits him to provide a decent living for his family will be seen as helpless to change the system without the united efforts of others — powerless in making demands of government or corporations. From this sense of powerlessness can come the motivation to join with others to overcome the injustice being experienced.

2. Realizing that material possessions are basic but not totally fulfilling, a person may begin to see that the quality of one's life is linked to the exercise of psychological, cultural, and spiritual rights and that devoting all one's energy and time to amassing great wealth is counterproductive.

3. Inner peace will grow within individuals as their awareness grows of their expanding utilization of their full right to human fulfillment. They will begin to appreciate a harmony between life as lived and its potential. Realizing that there is not perfect congruence, the individual is better able to face this reality and seek effective ways with others of improving the situation.

4. Reflection on one's rights can also enhance one's sense of personal dignity so that she or he will become able to participate in group action to bring about justice for others.

For your reflection:

What changes must you make in your life to be more fully human after the image of Jesus?

Questions for Reflection and Discussion

1. Consider carefully the scriptural meaning of truth. How have you experienced God's truth in your life?
2. Examine Merton's concept of truth. What does this concept mean to you in terms of your own life?
3. What similarities do you find in Gandhi's search for truth and your own search?
4. Do you believe that "truth-force" as used by Gandhi would be effective in unjust situations today? Why or why not?

5. What evidence do you see that we are moving toward deliberately choosing "the course that leads to destruction" in the world today?

6. Reflect on your own work experience. Are you aware of any dehumanizing aspects of your work, now or in the past? How have you responded to these injustices?

7. Make a list of human rights and indicate next to each one the degree to which you can exercise this right — fully, adequately, somewhat, not at all.

8. What changes must you make in your life to be more fully human after the image of Jesus?

Reading III
PEACE: BUILT ON JUSTICE

Section 1

. . . you have been . . . justified in the name of our Lord Jesus . . .

1 Corinthians 6:11

The person who earnestly seeks the truth by striving to become more human after the manner of Jesus sooner or later reaches a moment of decision. It then becomes clear to her or to him that for continued growth in integrity reflection alone is not enough — that it is necessary to move into action.

Reflection serves to bring to light two areas where action is necessary. The truth-seeker comes first to the realization that oppression, coming from *outside forces,* limits any achievement of full humanity; and then, in honesty, will be brought to admit that there are weaknesses and tendencies to evil *within the heart* of the seeker itself. If true peace is to be built on justice, both these areas need to be dealt with. The first requires works of justice, but the second makes even greater demands on the individual. It necessitates becoming a just person.

Justice, like peace, is both a gift and the result of human struggle. Isaiah pictures justice descending from heaven like dew. It will become fruitful when it is received as gift (Isaiah 45:8). Paul adds another aspect of justice when he tells us that it is a gift that we can receive because of the saving power of Jesus (Romans 5:17). Both Isaiah and Paul are saying that God offers all people the gift of justice, but we must reach out and accept the gift.

Unfortunately, we find it very difficult to be open to the gift God so freely offers. This resistance comes from our sinfulness and is part of our human condition. We can try to evade our responsibility by denying that we have the freedom to make choices or by stating that our environment and heredity determine our responses to life, but we are only deluding ourselves. This reluctance on the part of the modern person to admit sin is not a recent development; as Karl Menninger has pointed out, this evasion is part of human history.

Since Vatican II the Church has been reexamining the meaning of human sinfulness. In *The Church in the Modern World* (sometimes also referred to by its original Latin title, *Gaudium et Spes,* or by the title given to it by another translator, *The Church Today*), the Council Fathers point out that a human being knows from experience inclinations to evil and recognizes evil in the world, a condition which did not come from a good Creator. One feels that the path to fulfillment is somehow blocked. One experiences both the call to transcendence and the pull downward to utter misery. When the true relationship with God is disrupted one becomes "out of harmony with himself, with others and all created things. Therefore man is split within himself. As a result, all of human life, whether individual or collective, shows itself to be a dramatic struggle between good and evil . . . " (*The Church in the Modern World*).

By reflecting on one's experience of relationship with God, one can come to a deeper understanding of sin. God is present in human existence and is experienced as the One who calls the person to transcend self, to move to the future, to go beyond the present situation. God's call is basically asking each one to act as he does and in keeping with the modeling of this activity which he has given us in Jesus. God's call to individuals is always a call to wholeness, to greater freedom, and so to greater humanness. The Church today, aware of advances in psychology, sees that human beings are moving toward a deeper development of personality and a fuller awareness of human rights. To recognize one's rights and duties and to act in accord with that recognition is not merely in keeping with the thrust of our intellectual and ethical lives but is, at the same time, a positive response to God, to the inner call of God active in our history.

Response to God is more than an answer, it is a reply which is a first step in commitment. When we respond to the call of God to greater freedom we are moved to commit ourselves to living with greater humanity. The simplest response one can give God is a "Yes" to the events, opportunities, and activities of life which contribute to greater authenticity. Sin, then, can be viewed as saying "No" to God's call to greater humanness and wholeness. Sin is more than just a simple act; it is a turning away from the path to commitment to God and his way. Sin reveals the inner attitude of the individual which is "sinful" in that it is not directed toward God. It is this basic sinfulness, this total personal orientation, that the modern person is becoming aware of and is often ambivalent about owning.

Every sin, in one sense, is both individual and social in its implications. Individually, a person who refuses to respond to God's call is weakening his or her relationship with God and is rejecting the opportunity to live more fully. But by the same act the power of sin in the world is increased as well. The power of sin can be understood as the influence or atmosphere of evil that results from sin. A person does not exist alone but is always in relationship to others and to the world. One comes into the world where the effects of sin are already operative and choices are influenced by the sinful environment in which one finds oneself. Although each person is free (knowing that different behavior is possible), one experiences this sinful environment as a power drawing away from responsible choices. Each subsequent sin adds to the power of sin in the world; because through habituation the sinner finds it personally more difficult to respond positively to God's call, and through social impact greater difficulties are created for others.

In terms of the pursuit of truth, each sin is a choice to live in untruth and to forego the possibility of greater personal peace. By increasing the power of sin in the world, each sin adds as well to the difficulty and complexity of strengthening world peace.

It would appear that the very search for truth, a person's striving to become authentic, does not produce peace in the human heart but, rather, just the opposite. One becomes restless, gets in touch with the lack of harmony within self. One sees this imbalance as affecting relationships with others and feels a sense of separation from all of creation. The more one struggles to overcome these imbalances by striving for greater humanity, the more one realizes the need for reconciliation — the need to render the thrust of his or her life other than self-centered. Given the power of sin in the world, some force or energy is needed to combat this power and make it possible for a person to act with greater love. Reconciliation attempts to do just that — to break through sinful and evil forces and free the individual for a more authentic response to God, for a more loving relationship with others, and a more reverent attitude toward material creation.

The Old Testament story of Joseph shows how reconciliation with God can transform relationships between people. Joseph had suffered injustice from his brothers, and reconciliation could not take place until there was evidence of their change of heart. Joseph saw in his brothers' concern for their father and their offering to remain in place of Benjamin a change in attitude. Their jealousy toward the father's favorite son and their resentment toward the father had been replaced by a loving, merciful caring. It is this attitude which appeals to Joseph's heart so strongly that he is able to reveal his identity to them and to respond to their desire for reconciliation.

In the New Testament, reconciliation with one's neighbor is a prerequisite to reconciliation with God. "If you bring your gift to the altar and there recall that your brother has anything against you, leave your gift at the altar, go first to be reconciled with your brother, and then come and offer your gift" (Matthew 5:23-24). The offering of a gift to God signifies the individual's desire to be reconciled to God. Paul makes it clear, however, that the whole process of reconciliation began with God. Through Christ, God reconciled us to himself "not counting men's transgressions against them" (2 Corinthians 5:19). It is not enough that God has reconciled us to himself in Christ and established a new order. We must respond in such a way that the reconciliation becomes effective in our lives. Our response must indicate a change of heart, saying "Yes" to

God's presence and action in our lives. It means taking on the attitude of Christ and being truly "in Christ," realizing that God has "entrusted the message of reconciliation to us" (2 Corinthians 5:19).

For your reflection:

How have you experienced reconciliation with God? with other people?

Section 2

**To do what is right and just
  is more acceptable to the LORD than sacrifice.**

Proverbs 21:3

Delivering the message of reconciliation involves more than telling the good news that we have been reconciled to God in Christ. Paul calls us "ambassadors for Christ" because God "has given us the ministry of reconciliation." (See 2 Corinthians 5:20 and 5:18.) This ministry is carried out through forgiveness and by healing the rupture of trust.

The restoration of trust between two individuals will demand that each so appreciates the good in the other that he or she seconds that other's internal sense of his or her own worth. The emphasis given earlier to the value of a conscious knowledge of one's dignity thus takes on a new dimension in reestablishing trust. In searching for truth the individual focuses primarily on those values and rights that develop a deeper sense of her or his own self-worth. In order to rebuild trust and bring about reconciliation, the minister of reconciliation must reach out to the other, reaffirming the other's basic sense of worth. This presupposes in the minister an inner sense of self-worth, which then gives the minister the security to affirm the other.

The ministry of reconciliation overcomes alienation between individuals. The necessity for this ministry in the world today can hardly be exaggerated. On any particular day, a glance at the headlines in the evening paper yields ample evidence of the presence of alienation in the world. A few of today's headlines read: "Black Leaders Feel Letdown," "Terrorist Holds Three Hostage," "Mail-Order Frauds Cost Americans One Billion," "Husband Convicted in Wife's Death." Each of these headlines merely highlights a situation in which people feel alienated and hurt. When such alienation becomes widespread a cultural pattern exists which cannot be changed by individual effort alone.

The Church is aware of this social phenomenon. Since the beginning of Vatican II the call to reconciliation has been issued through Church documents with an even greater insistence. Nine days after the Council opened, for the first time in the history of ecumenical councils, the Council Fathers addressed a message to all people. Their "Message to Humanity" reiterates the belief of the Church that the Father sent his Son to free us from the bondage of sin. It thus asserts that conciliation has already taken place, in fact, that peace has already become a reality as a gift from God. This implies that if we experience quite the contrary we are blocking God's activity and preventing God's gift from being effective.

The Church in the Modern World gives us practical, specific directives for bringing about reconciliation. Reconciliation must be founded on respect and love for all, even for those who think or act differently from the way in which we do in social, political, or religious matters. Going deeper than surface differences, without being indifferent to truth and goodness, we must love the person. In fact, our very love for the individual may make it necessary for us to speak the truth, to call the individual to correct errors; but only God can make judgments about the guilt of anyone. The teaching of Christ even requires that our reconciliation extend to loving and forgiving those who have harmed us, for he said, "You have heard the commandment, 'You shall love your countryman but hate your enemy.' My command to you is: love your enemies, pray for your persecutors" (Matthew 5:43-44).

Pope Paul VI, writing on the importance of reconciliation to peace, remarked: "It is not enough to contain wars, to suspend conflicts, to impose truces and armistices, to define boundaries and relationships, to create sources of common interest; it is not enough to paralyze the possibility of radical strife through the terror of unheard destruction and suffering. Progress must be made toward a peace founded on reconciliation of hearts" ("Reconciliation — the Way to Peace").

But breaking the bonds of sin is not all that is required to facilitate works on behalf of justice; psychological development must also take place. The individual must have moved to that level of consciousness at which world vision leads to works of justice: Going beyond the internalization of self-worth and dependence on the approval of others, self-direction must free the creative imagination. The world will then be seen as expanding, and challenge the individual to work to change it. In greater freedom of choice one will become sensitive to the rights of others and accept the responsibility of helping others own their rights. This sense of responsibility will be accompanied by a feeling of power within self to actually effect some change. Such a person will have "maturity."

The mature individual has the ability to focus on rights that go beyond his or her own individual needs. As a member of society one becomes aware of rights in relationship to others. If a person's own basic needs for food, clothing, shelter, rest, medical care, and necessary social services are being adequately met, then the person can move outward to the needs of others. These needs and the corresponding rights are so fundamental and so essential for the dignity of the individual that one cannot function in a human way without them. Psychologists have shown that only when primary physical needs are satisfied does a person seek intellectual and emotional fulfillment.

What does this tell us about the twenty-five percent of the human family that suffers from serious malnutrition? How could people living in subhuman conditions which do not even provide food possibly experience a sense of inner peace? If peace is the harmony between people's lives and their potential for a fully human life, how could they possibly experience inner peace? What these statistics establish is that at least one fourth of the human family is incapable of experiencing peace because they are deprived of the elements essential to making peace possible — they are denied the most basic human right, enough food for life and health.

The very existence of such populations sets up tensions between leaders of the have nations and the have-not nations and produces a climate hostile to world peace. The presence within a nation of hungry, starving people is also a threat to the peace of the nation. These people have a right to what they need to live a decent human life. If they attempt to take what they need because the suffering inflicted on them by the unjust economic system becomes unbearable, they are met with violence and greater oppression.

For your reflection:

In what way has reconciliation contributed to an experience of greater freedom in your life?

Section 3

This . . . is the fasting that I wish . . . sharing your bread with the hungry, sheltering the oppressed and the homeless. . . .
Isaiah 58:6,7

At the beginning of this reading, it was stated that the truth-seeker finds two kinds of limitations to freedom that demand action: (1) those one experiences within and (2) those resulting from outside forces. This second group is so vast that we will focus on one man's response and the impact of his sensitivity on the nations of the world.

When the United Nations Conference, Habitat '76, highlighted the inhuman conditions in which a large portion of humanity exists, Enrique Penalosa, the Colombian economist who was then secretary general, was largely responsible for its success.

As his immediate preparation for the Habitat meeting, Penalosa spent two years traveling throughout the world, studying human settlements. His interest was not in housing alone but in habitations in the broadest sense: the total environment necessary to human beings to live a decent life. He considered the basic services available, transportation facilities, opportunities for education, employment, and leisure-time activities.

Penalosa found that government housing agencies, in providing low income housing units, often make no provision for the lives of those inhabiting these dwellings. The high-rise housing projects of many U.S. cities, though well-intentioned, often gather many frustrated, unhappy people into one limited area where they have shelter but little more. The overcrowded conditions lessen the possibility of other needs being met.

In the eighty-five countries he visited, one of the worst areas was Hong Kong. There even the drug problem seemed to pale by comparison to the housing crisis: in one area there were 400,000 people per square mile, with the majority of families existing in one room, in squatter huts, or in rooftop shacks. In spite of the 1.8 million dwellings provided by the government, there were approximately 300,000 people with no accommodations.

However, Penalosa found that conditions in Latin America were the worst in the world. Worse even than in India where, in Calcutta alone, a quarter of a million people are born, live, and die in the streets, since in India only ten percent of the population live in large cities. A much larger percentage of Latin Americans already live in urban areas, and the numbers will increase dramatically during the remainder of the century unless something is done to reverse the trend.

In spite of all the interlocking problems involved in providing adequate housing for the world's people — in such a way that total human development is taken into account — there is hope engendered by the very fact that the whole human family is now concerned. Representatives from many nations are now talking together about their problems of supplying food and shelter for all their citizens. The recognition of these problems as too big for any one nation gives a sense that we are all involved in a common problem.

Habitat '76 had no legislative power, so could only make recommendations which, of necessity, had to be rather general. Every country was urged to have a national policy on human settlements, dealing with population distribution and related social and economic problems. The conference members realized that there are widely differing standards of living in countries throughout the world, and recommended that housing take into account the culture and local resources. Other recommendations dealt with land ownership, use of land, patterns of ownership, planning of services, and management of institutions. Such a comprehensive approach calls for *public* participation, and the conference did not hesitate to encourage such involvement.

From this consideration of the basic right to decent living conditions, it seems apparent that the solutions to injustices are not simple. In a complex society such as exists today, there are no simple answers to life's problems. The less obvious conclusion to be drawn from what has been said is the type of action called for from the individual. There are so many circumstances involved in this choice. Qualities of the individual such as temperament, physical stamina, fears, interests, level of trust, ability to analyze, and organizational skills enter into the picture. Also, the practical questions of availability of time, transportation, health, and resources will limit one's choices. Other factors, such as particular needs of the locale, needs not being met in other ways, the possibility of assistance from others, and funding must also be assessed. Discernment is needed on the part of the individual to deal with all these factors and to reach a viable decision.

Care should be taken, however, not to become so engrossed in the factors involved in the choice that no choice is ever made. It seems apparent that action is crucial if an individual is striving for authenticity and reconciliation. The often quoted statement of the Synod of Bishops in 1971, "Action on behalf of justice and participation in the transformation of the world fully appear to us as a constitutive dimension of the preaching of the Gospel, or, in other words, of the Church's mission for the redemption of the human race and its liberation from every oppressive situation," challenges us to some kind of action. And the bishops went on to give an important guideline that helps to focus our choices. They said, "Our action is to be directed at those people and nations which, because of various forms of oppression and because of the present character of our society are silent, indeed voiceless, victims of injustice" (*Justice in the Modern World*).

For your reflection:

What are some of the factors that will influence your choice of action for justice?

Section 4

Let us love in deed and in truth and not merely talk about it.
1 John 3:18

God is always active in his creation, but his action strikes the thinking Christian most forcibly when an ordinary incident, because of its time and circumstances, becomes significant. Such an incident took place in Montgomery, Alabama, on December 1, 1955.

Racial discrimination was a fact of life. There was nothing unusual about a black woman being told to relinquish her seat on the bus to a white passenger. What was different was that Mrs. Rosa Parks refused to move. What was the spark that motivated her? Was it a sense of her own dignity? A conviction that she had as much right to that seat as anyone else? A smoldering resentment from all that she had suffered from whites? A retaliation for some particular injustice she had suffered in the recent past? Whatever her motivation, the fact was that she *did* refuse to move and was arrested. Innumerable blacks had been arrested in Montgomery over the years without any repercussions, but this time things began to happen. Her courage lighted sparks in other hearts ready to act against oppression and a bus boycott resulted. Martin Luther King Jr. led the boycott to a successful conclusion. It was the beginning of a new stage in the black struggle for justice.

Martin Luther King Jr. was only twenty-six years old at the time. At this point in his life he was committed to two courses of action: (1) the elimination of racial injustice and (2) the use of nonviolent means in order to accomplish this end. The bus boycott in Montgomery thrust him into a leadership position at a time when he was ready to assume that burden. He saw clearly that the injustices suffered by his people were expressions of one basic social fact: segregation. His philosophy of social action had become equally clear, so that after the boycott he could tell the white people of the city that their violence would be met with even stronger nonviolence. He planned to overcome the evil of segregation by the nonviolent resistance of rallies, marches, and political strategies.

* * * * *

Betty Williams in Northern Ireland likewise began her work for justice in response to an incident. On August 10, the driver of an IRA getaway car was shot. The car went out of control, jumped the curb, and crushed to death three young children, ages eight, two, and six weeks. Betty Williams, the wife of a marine engineer and mother of two children, who lived several blocks from the scene of the accident, was shocked into "declaring war on war." She went from door to door talking to people of the neighborhood, begging them to join her in protesting the senseless killings. She led two hundred people in a march into Andersonstown, the Catholic ghetto, where she was joined by Mairead Corrigan, the aunt of the three dead children.

Instead of reacting with bitterness, Mairead spoke from the depths of her faith. She saw the deaths of the three children as a sign that was not to be forgotten. She recognized it as a personal call for her to work for peace. She went on TV and condemned the IRA. No one had dared to speak out with such courage since 1970. Together, she and Betty had 30,000 Catholics and Protestants marching for peace after just two weeks.

On the third march in late August, the Catholic women dared to cross the dividing line into Protestant territory. Instead of being met by violence their ranks were swelled by Protestant women, among them Nancy McDonnell who was to become one of Betty's staunchest friends. It seems that people were just waiting and hoping for leadership, for after only four months there were 500 to 20,000 marching each weekend in different towns. A magazine, *Peace by Peace,* was being published, two offices were established, and 120 groups were in operation. By December 1976, the group had decided on two strategies: weekly Saturday marches and small group meetings between Catholics and Protestants to talk out their differences and common concerns. At the end of eight months there were 8,000 members of the Community of Peace People, Catholics and Protestants, unionists and Republicans. They had gathered 300,000 signatures for peace.

Two years later, there was still fighting going on in Northern Ireland, the number of active Peace People had declined, and one heard little of Betty and Mairead. In an interview in the summer of 1977, Betty and Nancy explained recent developments. Although the number of members in the Community had declined from 8,000 to approximately 100, Betty was not discouraged but attributed this decline to the fact that the charismatic phase was over and the work for building a peaceful society had begun. Instead of concentrating on one area of injustice, she was providing the leadership to attack the causes and consequences of violence in Northern Ireland. She called upon the people to participate in community politics and work together for solutions to the high rate (thirty-eight to forty-one percent) of unemployment. At the same time she was attempting to alleviate the unfortunate consequences suffered by many who live in a violent society. Violence in the streets often finds its counterpart of violence in the home, and there is a tremendous problem of battered wives and abused children in Ireland. Shelters have been established in several cities for the care and protection of the victims of violence in the home.

* * * * *

Rehabilitation centers have also been set up in urban areas for boys coming out of prison. Young boys, both Catholic and Protestant, are victimized by the fighting. Because of the extremely high rate of unemployment, they are easily drawn into one of the nine military organizations. When captured by an opposing force they are frequently crippled before being released, to guarantee that they will not fight again. When they come out of prison they need the physical and psychological care provided at the rehabilitation centers. While not as dramatic as massive peace marches, the work Betty and the members of the Community of Peace People are doing is just as important, if not more significant, in bringing about peace.

* * * * *

In summary, the truth-seeker comes to know that the achievement of a peaceful heart is impossible without effective action for justice. Greater inner harmony is seen to flow from an honest admission of one's sinfulness and a sincere desire for reconciliation with God and with others. Reconciliation with others involves reestablishing trust, helping the other to experience again his or her own dignity and self-worth. This reconciliation is impossible without some success in removing those injustices which force people to live in dehumanizing conditions. It becomes evident, then, that struggling for justice increases the inner peace of the contender and, at the same time, brings about a more ordered and harmonious society. What we have not yet considered is motivation of the whole process by charity, the bond that cements together into a community those working for the same goal.

For your reflection:

"Action on behalf of justice is a constitutive dimension of preaching the Gospel." What action for justice are you integrating into your life?

Questions for Reflection and Discussion

1. How do you understand the relationship between justice, individual sin, and the leading of a more fully human life?
2. In what way can it be said that individual sin is also social sin?

3. How have you experienced reconciliation with God? with other people?
4. In what way has reconciliation contributed to an experience of greater freedom in your life?
5. Do you believe that programs such as Habitat '76 are effective in bringing about societal change? Why or why not? What disadvantages does such a program have?
6. What are some of the circumstances that will influence your action for justice?
7. "Action on behalf of justice is a constitutive dimension of preaching the Gospel." What action for justice are you integrating into your life?

Reading IV
PEACE: MOTIVATED AND INTEGRATED BY CHARITY

Section 1

Love does not rejoice in what is wrong but rejoices with the truth.

1 Corinthians 13:6

The truth-seeker who has become a justice-builder faces, before very long, the challenges and feelings of disappointment that can grow into disgust for the whole undertaking and contempt for those who apparently refuse to be helped. It is precisely at this point that the individual becomes deeply aware of the need for the support and encouragement of a community.

Much has been written on community in the past ten years, and different authors have defined community from their own perspective. Certain elements, however, seem to be basic in any definition: (1) individuals, (2) a common bond uniting the individuals, and (3) a group resulting from this union. In each case, the community is made up of individuals, each with unique talents, personality, gifts, and skills.

This very uniqueness of the individuals, however, tends to isolate and segregate each from the others. Before a community is possible, therefore, some common bond must draw the individuals together. This common bond not only unites individuals but somehow forms a living entity with distinct qualities of its own. Persons bonded together by a common goal, interest, or policy form a community which is more than the sum of the individuals. The community, having its own life, can grow, develop, and mature, or it can decay, regress, or disintegrate. The life of a community can be so apparent that an individual loves the community as a friend, looks to it for love and support, challenges it to greater life, grieves for its sorrows in the same way as one reacts to a close friend. One does all this not because one has been taught to act this way nor because of a felt obligation; the heart knows that this living, vital entity is valuable and worthy of love and loyalty.

Obviously, not every community brings forth this response from its individual members. There are many levels of community, depending on the bond linking individuals. There is a bond linking members of a baseball team or a Mafia family or players in a bridge club. So, in one sense, each group might be called a community. However, to be a peace-promoting community demands a much stronger bond between the members.

Josiah Royce, an American philosopher writing in the early twentieth century, maintains that love must be the bond of community when he says: "A community must be a union of members who first love it." He presents us with a paradox when he goes on to say: "The unity of love must pervade it before the individual member can find it lovable. Yet unless the individuals first love it, how can the unity of love come to pervade it?" (*The Problem of Christianity*) The way out of what might appear as a vicious circle lies in the influence of a leader who embodies the goals and interests of the community. The leader must be strong enough to declare and witness to the existence of a bond of love uniting the leader to still disparate and isolated individuals. It takes a leader with vision to recognize the existence of such a bond and to make it visible for others. It is, therefore, true to say that the life of the community first exists within the leader and becomes a living entity only after the birth struggle of bringing it forth for others.

The implications of this discussion for those who are working against injustices are many. Seeking support from those with the same awareness of injustices and the same determination to remedy the situation is not enough. There is a bond of interest which draws the individuals together, but this bond is not strong enough to withstand the frustrations, disappointments, and failures one meets in any struggle against oppression and injustice. What is needed is to belong to a loving community that is a group bonded together by love in its common desire to help others. The motivation is no longer sought in the cooperation, gratitude, and good will of those being served, but the motivational power comes from the love found in community, a love which must first exist in the heart of a loving leader.

The English language is not particularly conducive to a deeper understanding of "motivation by love" in that it does not readily distinguish between the various kinds of love. The Greeks had three words for love: *eros, philia,* and *agape.* Each word signifies a different quality or aspect of love. *Eros* is used to refer to romantic or aesthetic love which has different expectations and charac-teristics from *philia,* a reciprocal love between friends. *Agape,* in the Christian sense, is a share in the love with which God loves all persons. As such, it is unbounded and extends to enemies as well as friends. *Agape* is the love that makes it possible to love the very one who causes you harm, to love one's enemies while, at the same time, not condoning or approving the wrong being done. *Agape* is a gift from God, a gift that God gives most readily to those who earnestly desire and pray for it. It is the love Paul describes so well:

> Love is patient; love is kind. Love is not jealous, it does not put on airs, it is not snobbish. Love is never rude, it is not self-seeking, it is not prone to anger; neither does it brood over injuries. Love does not rejoice in what is wrong but rejoices with the truth. There is no limit to love's forbearance, to its trust, its hope, its power to endure (1 Corinthians 13:4-7).

It is this kind of love that inspires a person to continue the war for justice against all odds.

For your reflection:

Reflect on the various communities to which you belong — on their membership, their goals, and the bond uniting the members. Which communities are most important in your life? Which one has exerted the greatest influence on you?

_____

Section 2

Let us profess the truth in love and grow to the full maturity of Christ the head.

Ephesians 4:15

What happens, then, to the individual who finds and joins a loving community? The person becomes part of a group and begins to experience what this means in personal development. One finds that when a group of persons actually forms a loving community some interesting dynamics take place. If each member accepts some past events that are also accepted by fellow members, the community takes on a quality that could lead to its being characterized, in Royce's terms, as a "community of memory." The memory of these past events which all share, actually or vicariously, becomes a common memory. It strengthens the bond of love and draws the community closer together. It is interesting to note also that the vitality of a community depends on the ability of its members to incorporate into their lives past events, even some so far in the past that the members have no personal memory of them. By accepting these events of the distant past the individual becomes more deeply rooted in the life of the community. This process is going on all the time as individuals accept the traditions and heritage of Church, country, family, and other communities. Without consciously realizing it the individual grows in inner peace through this community of memory, for his grasp of truth is reinforced by the witness of others sharing the same truth.

Of perhaps greater significance to the advocate of justice are the dynamics involved in the development of a community's orientation toward the future. A community shares dreams of the future and makes plans to bring some of its dreams to reality. As each member personally makes the same expected future events his own, as his fellow members do, a deeper bond is formed. Their common expectations of the future not only act as a further bond between the individual members but are, as well, an explicit call to action for the group: each member being committed to passing on the dream and to cooperating in achieving it. As each member works to accomplish the goal and observes fellow members doing the same, each one begins to realize that it is only through this orderly interaction of individuals that the community is able to accomplish what no one of them could do alone. The completed task is seen as more than the sum of the individual efforts. Added cooperation and the complementarity of efforts give to community activity a new dimension. At the same time, each member feels the support of the group and shares in the feeling of accomplishment. This is not to say that all the difficulties and struggles of striving for justice vanish, but the problems become less formidable when those striving for justice are motivated by love and each one experiences the concern and support of the community.

We can get a better sense of a loving community by considering the apostolic community. Luke tells us:

They [the first Christians] devoted themselves to the apostles' instruction and communal life, to the breaking of bread and the prayers. . . . Those who believed shared all things in common; they would sell their property and goods, dividing everything on the basis of each one's need. They went to the temple area together every day, while in their homes they broke bread. With exultant and sincere hearts they took their meals in common, praising God and winning the approval of all the people (Acts 2:42-47).

The author's understanding of the basis of this sharing is significant. Luke mentions that the early Christians were united in faith and in the desire to grow in their faith by learning more about Jesus, by praying together, and participating in the Eucharist. Being bonded by love into a community of memory they were motivated to share on a material level so that no one in the community was in need. It is important to note that the bond holding the community together was faith in Jesus and love for both Christ and all those he loves. The sharing on a material level was a consequence of the love they had for one another. The sharing of resources was the outward expression of the love already present in their hearts, a love first of all for Jesus and secondarily for those he loves.

A statement that succinctly describes the prevailing attitude of the apostolic community is Luke's description, "The community of believers were of one heart and one mind" (Acts 4:32). It is apparent from the events narrated in Acts that being of one mind did not mean that there were no differences among the early Christians. We know that the question of receiving Gentiles into the Church without their first becoming Jews caused dissension, and that Paul and Barnabas disagreed sharply about taking John Mark to visit the Gentile churches. It seems, rather, that being of one mind signifies the common faith they all professed in the risen Lord. This faith was so strong that it could survive arguments and disagreements so that the community was not split apart by the discord. Living Paul's injunction to the Philippians, "Your attitude must be that of Christ," they were able to work out their differences (Philippians 2:5). The bond of community held them together in their hardships and trials. Being of one heart they loved one another and could continue to communicate and to arrive at solutions to their problems. When some of the Christians in Jerusalem took issue with Peter for entering the house of uncircumcised men and eating with them, Peter explained his thinking to them. Their love and respect for Peter gave them the openness to listen to him, to search for the truth of his words, and to respond in freedom. In the words of Luke, "When they heard this they stopped objecting, and instead began to glorify God in these words: 'If this be so, then God has granted life-giving repentance even to the Gentiles'" (Acts 11:18). This event highlights the communication that is necessary if a community, once formed, is not to disintegrate through dissension and misunderstandings which shatter the inner peace of individual members.

Communication is so necessary to the birth, development, and maturing of community that Rollo May does not hesitate to define community simply as a group that engages in open conversation.

The fact that we use words with the same root to signify the group of individuals united and bonded together and the method of expressing ideas and feelings within the group is no coincidence: *communication* is more than talking to another or carrying on a conversation. It is relaying to another by means of words, symbols, and body language the thoughts and feelings in one's mind and heart. It is being true to one's self in the presence of the other person and allowing that person to share the image one has of one's self. To be true communication the second person must accept without judgment the self he sees before him and be willing to share himself in response. When this authentic communication takes place each is in touch with the humanity of the other and grows in understanding of the other and the self. Inner desires to manipulate, to dominate are no longer a felt necessity in order to defend oneself, for one sees the other as also vulnerable. When empty dialogue is replaced by true communication the oppressor and the oppressed will both be seeking the truth in the situation and will not be trying to take advantage of the other. Only then will negotiations for peaceful living become fruitful.

For your reflection:

Compare the early Christian community described by Luke to the parish community today. What can you do to make your parish a more Christian community reflecting the values of the apostolic community?

Section 3

Where two or three are gathered in my name, there am I in their midst.

Matthew 18:20

Lest we think that this portrait of the apostolic community is too idealistic for modern people to imitate, Sheila Cassidy witnesses to such a community which she experienced in a Chilean prison. She writes in her autobiography:

In the early days . . . the prisoners kept the gifts brought by their relations until it was recognized that the families of some of the prisoners were in such straitened circumstances that they were going hungry themselves in order to bring food for their daughter or wife. It was decided, therefore, to pool all the provisions that were brought and redistribute them according to the needs of the prisoners. The sharing of food gradually extended to include a sharing of toilet articles among the inhabitants of the different rooms. . . . It was soon found that a common pool of clothes was essential as all new prisoners arrived only in the clothes in which they had been detained and they were always desperately in need of clean ones. . . . The greatest triumph in community living was achieved when it was decided to share cigarettes (*Audacity to Believe*).

We sense the deep commitment to one another and the generous love motivating the sharing in such difficult circumstances. The closing sentence of the quotation reveals the challenge to the individual and the high expectations each had of the others. Sheila writes, " . . . each week one girl was nominated the 'economist' and anyone who was hungry between meals had to ask permission of the economist for a biscuit or other snack and on the one occasion when someone helped herself without asking, the community was deeply shocked." What is truly remarkable about this prison community is that a significant number of the members were not Christians but were nonbelievers and Marxists. How does one explain the mystery of the love, a love which so obviously has qualities of the love of Christ's heart, which motivates these people?

Considered from a psychological viewpoint, the same pattern emerges in believing and nonbelieving communities: As an individual reaches a deeper level of consciousness and sees the need for action to overcome some of the injustice in the world, that person seeks to communicate these insights to others. The individual has become more aware of individual rights and perceives that these rights are not always attainable in our technological society. The person experiences within self a desire to express this newly found awareness to others and to share ideas and feelings of powerlessness. Often this vision is met with apathy, boredom, disagreement, or even hostility; and the response to the reaction of others at this point is crucial.

When attempts at communication are met with rebuffs, the temptation is present to doubt the truth within. One may be haunted by the question, "Why do I feel the injustices of the world so strongly when others don't seem to care? Is there something wrong with my perception of reality?" If the person withdraws, even psychologically, at this point, no further growth will take place. Then action on behalf of justice is possible, but it will be some form of unilateral endeavor. For example, one may give a contribution to an organization sending food to the hungry of India or give some cast-off clothing to the Thanksgiving clothing drive. These are good projects and may be emergency measures, but they must be recognized for what they are — emergency measures. They are necessary because we have not yet gotten to the root of the problem, the sinful social structures that condemn vast numbers of people to poverty and starvation.

Participating in emergency measures has a built-in frustration which can be healthy. Knowing that radical solutions are needed, that new patches on old problems are inadequate at best, one has a sense of helplessness and frustration. What one does with these feelings will determine, to a large extent, one's growth in consciousness. Nursing the frustration and sinking into self-pity only lead to inaction in the future and rejection of the truth of one's humanity. It is impossible to live in today's world and not be aware at times of injustice, oppression, violence, and cruelty. Not to be willing to move beyond the feeling of frustration only condemns a person to deliberate illusions and a twisting of truth to alleviate the discomfort.

To react in a healthy way to the experience of frustration means to seek to alleviate the discomfort by taking the realistic and optimistic attitude that there are others somewhere who have the same perception of truth. It is only necessary to search for them by continuing to communicate and hope for a response that will make this sharing mutual. When that hope has been realized, that is, when one discovers others who see the injustice and together they seek ways of responding, the possibility of a community exists.

For your reflection:

Show from your own experiences the importance of open communication in relationships and community living.

Section 4

**Your young men shall see visions
and your old men shall dream dreams.**

Acts 2:17

In Roger Schutz we find an example of a leader who embodied the love that would blossom into a loving community with an outward thrust toward justice. While still in theological studies, Roger became leader of a discussion group which tried to find solutions to the individualism its members experienced in the Angelican Church. He saw the danger of divorcing his own private spiritual life from involvement with people needing his love and care.

Being a leader motivated by love he soon drew others together into a loving community. Two young men joined him, and, from their discussions and common discernment, a spirituality developed which took form in a rule. Slowly a decision took shape among them that they express their trust in God's faithfulness by committing themselves for life to God and the service of others. The first seven Brothers had come from different countries and belonged to different churches, but they had learned to look at their common bonds rather than at the dissimilarities. They had come to believe that their living together would give outward expression to the power of Christ to bring about unity. And so the community of Taizé came into existence. Even today, after forty years of experience, one of the chief characteristics of the community is its unanimity in plural-ism.

From all levels of society men with widely divergent back-grounds, education, and professional training began joining the group. Because their primary aim is service to the world no one has been ordained to minister to the community, although the several ministers who have joined the group continue their ministry. The Brothers are deeply concerned about problems of injustice, hun-ger, poverty, and oppression; and are prepared for work in this area by studying sociology during the time of their initial formation. Small groups have gone to South Africa, to Algeria, and to the factories of France to share the life of the poor and to learn firsthand what can be done to alleviate the social evils. Once a year all the Brothers return to Taizé to share experiences and get a deeper insight into their work and its effects.

The Brothers do not make a vow of poverty, but, rather, they renounce all title to property and promise to share material goods in community. In giving up ownership of material goods the Brothers do not strive to be poor, for poverty is not looked upon as a good. They work not only for their own sustenance but also to have resources to share with the poor. From the very beginning the Brothers invested their surplus in projects that were socially pro-ductive. At first, the community took care of war orphans and, later, started a dairy cooperative to help the people of their area. In 1961, Prior Schutz heeded the suggestion of Pope John that rural families organize themselves into cooperatives. The community owns soil, equipment, and machinery in common with five families of the area. All profits are shared on the basis of the amount of work contributed by each. The fact that the community has no exclusive title to land or equipment means that it shares the ups and downs of the economy with its neighbors. They do not live in secure isolation from the farmers of the area. In this way their concerns are identi-fied with those of their rural neighbors.

Yet, the Brothers see themselves primarily as a community which shares its spiritual rather than material goods. They strive earnestly for an openness and transparency of the whole person, first in their relationships with one another and then in their corporate ministry. This sharing of spiritual goods finds expression in the unique openness with which the community shares its life. Every day throughout the summer and early fall, streams of people pour into Taizé to share in the community's prayer and at its table. Some of the Brothers are always available to talk to visitors, to answer their questions, and to witness to a life of love and sharing. The Brothers also organize work communities in which young men share in their work and their prayer and study for a short time. At the end of the period the young men make a retreat, ending in a commitment to participate in assisting the poor to realize their human dignity. Through those who were once members of such work communities the spirit of Taizé is spread throughout the world.

The Brothers not only receive thousands of pilgrims at Taizé but they form temporary communities in areas of human misery or divisiveness as well. There they live in rented dwellings with only the bare necessities, while several of the group find jobs to support the others who give retreats, hold meetings, and organize groups to work for social reform. The witness of those working in factories, driving trucks, or performing unskilled labor is considered of equal importance to that of those giving retreats or doing organizational work for justice. Such action on behalf of the poor of the world flows from the ecumenical thrust of the community of Taizé. The unity they strive for is not merely a *unity of* all Christians but is a *unity for* the purpose of bringing the Gospel to all unbelievers.

"Operation Hope" is a related continuing program of larger scope. At the invitation of South American bishops, this program was organized to provide peasants with the tools and training required for cooperative farming. The peasants are helped to form small communities and to utilize methods derived from the experience of the Taizé cooperative. "Operation Hope" is ecumenical; and all peasants, regardless of religion, are eligible to take part. Since the International Week of Prayer for Unity in 1963, funds are solicited from all Christians who are interested in ecumenism.

In "Operation Hope" can be seen the fruitfulness of a community of peace: The divisiveness caused by economic inequality is being healed, and the dignity of the poor is safeguarded as they are given the means to help themselves and to learn from one another. As the Brothers give they also receive from the peasants a greater sense of God's providence. It is through such solidarity that the Gospel of peace becomes credible and Christians begin to be aware of the possibility of unity.

* * * * *

Another work for peace and justice organized by the community, which has had far-reaching and profound effects, was the Council of Youth in 1974. Planning for the Council began as early as 1969. The community was faced with the challenge of planning a project which would do several things: (1) assist youth in its search for peace; (2) lead them to a commitment to Christ; and (3) release their youthful energies and creativity to change the hatred and violence of the world into peace.

After the announcement of the Council on Easter 1970, a time of intensive preparation began without anyone knowing how long the preparation would take. The preparation for the Council of Youth did not follow the usual easy way of preparing for a large international meeting. There were no meetings to draw up proposals, no assemblies or congresses. The Council was not to be a series of inspiring talks or lectures exhorting youth to change their lives with the expectation that they return to their own countries and live out the exhortations. Rather, the Council was to be a sharing of experiences of living lives dedicated to service during the time of preparation.

Many youths found it difficult to understand what was expected of them before the Council. It was most difficult for the young people of the First World to live with the ambiguity of "living the Joyful News" in preparation for sharing this experience at the Council. They wanted first a blueprint of how the Council was to be organized and guidelines and directives for preparation. Instead they were told to look within themselves, to let the Joyful News penetrate them and liberate them from within.

Young people from all over the world united in small groups to prepare for the Council. Some went to Taizé for several weeks in the summer and returned home fired with enthusiasm to get others involved in the preparations. Gradually, they became aware of the broader aspects of justice, and called one another to accept responsibility for changing not only their own hearts but the structures which were keeping so many in oppression.

As a result of all this preparation, 40,000 young people from 120 countries gathered in Taizé in late summer 1974. They discussed the world's needs and the Church's mission. As a follow-up, a team went with the Prior to Calcutta, India, and Chittagong, Bangladesh. They spent several weeks serving the poor, the suffering, and the dying, praying and reflecting together. As a result of that experience they wrote a "Second Letter to the People of God" which was read at an ecumenical service in Notre Dame, Paris.

This "Letter" called upon the People of God to witness to a new future for all. In it, the Council of Youth representatives challenged all the People of God to divest themselves, gradually, over a seven-year period, of everything that is not essential. They asked them to eliminate from their lives the competition for better jobs motivated by the one desire of making more money. They asked them to resist the urge to accumulate wealth and to open their homes in hospitality to others.

These idealistic youths realized the risks involved; they recognized the need for new sources of energy to take those risks. These they had discovered in the experience of preparing themselves for the Council and in their work together in Asia. They were convinced that the source is the love to be found in prayer, especially prayer with Scripture, wherein the word of Jesus touches one's heart and moves the person to action.

For your reflection:

Do you feel that the challenges of the young people in the "Second Letter to the People of God" are realistic? What would happen if a significant number of people accepted these challenges? Are you willing to accept them?

Section 5

Through him the whole body grows, and with the proper functioning of the members joined firmly together by each supporting ligament, builds itself up in love.

Ephesians 4:16

A community that has been living the risks proposed at Taizé for some years is the House of Daybreak in Seoul, Korea. The community grew from a series of lectures given by Dr. Moon Dong Whan (*not* the founder of the "moonie" movement in America). Dr. Moon, called Stephen Moon by his Western friends, was pastor of a Presbyterian Church in Seoul in 1971 when he became concerned about the materialistic, competitive life-style of many Christians. He began to develop, in talks to his parishioners, the ideal of a life free from consumerism, a life based on human values and communal sharing; and some of those parishioners were inspired to explore the realities of such a way of life.

Four families and two single persons pledged themselves to try community living for at least six months with the option of renewing the covenant each subsequent year. They agreed to share everything; and soon discovered, as many communities have, that sharing material resources was the simplest part of the sharing. What emerged as the most difficult part was the sharing of themselves through relating openly and honestly with the other members of the community. They found they could not do this without constant communication, so they set up weekly meetings to work out their problems.

Unlike some groups who have come together for their own personal good, the House of Daybreak did so out of concern for the larger community. With this in mind, they decided to budget their expenses to the wages of a limited number of the group, so that the others might be freed to work for the poor and disadvantaged. They opened a kindergarten for the poor children of the neighborhood and formed a support group of older "second wives" who, according to Korean law, have no legal rights, are often mistreated by their husbands, and are looked down upon by society.

In keeping with the Confessing Church model of Dietrich Bonhoeffer, the House of Daybreak aims at the integration of worship and action for justice. They are outspoken against the oppression of the government and from the beginning have been monitored by the Korean CIA. Several members of the community, including the founder, Steve, have been fired from their jobs because of their opposition to the injustices under which they live.

After the community had been together for some time, their interest became more and more focused on organic farming, and they decided to move to the country in order to help small farmers in their struggle to make a living. They hoped to develop and provide a model that would enable farmers to free themselves from ever greater impoverishment by the wealthy. This move to the farm provided unexpected challenges since their whole way of living had to be rethought and adjusted to the demands of farming.

The many tensions created by the move were aggravated by the arrest of Steve, his older brother, and sixteen friends. These prominent Koreans had signed a statement criticizing the oppressive tactics of the government and calling for a restoration of democracy. They were arrested, and Steve had to serve a three-year prison term. His absence at such a crucial time for the community was keenly felt by the rest of the members, but they continued to struggle for greater peace and harmony among themselves and for justice in Korea.

* * * * *

The communities of Taizé and Seoul are very different and have had very different roots, but they share some of the qualities of the apostolic community. They see the necessity of a sharing not only of material things but more importantly a sharing of talents, of intellectual gifts, and especially of spiritual goods. Although neither of these groups united specifically to struggle and strive for justice, they have both grown in this direction. The outward expression of the desire to meet the needs of others has been very different, but each has contributed in its own way to world peace.

The House of Daybreak, although it is a small community, is having an impact on injustice in Korea. Its members themselves are acquiring, through their struggles to adjust to living on the farm, an inner peace and with it the strength and courage to speak out on behalf of justice in the face of consequences. They are finding in the bond that unites them the fortitude they need to resist an oppressive government.

In each of these communities we find individuals bonded together in love, a love that does not remain within the boundaries of the community. The living entity, which is the community, becomes a powerhouse of love greater than the love of all the separate individuals. This overflow of love goes out to the poor, the needy, the deprived, in any way, in an effective surge. It also gives support and courage to the individuals of the community, freeing them from their doubts and fears, to do more than they believed possible. In each case we find that this love is really a sharing in the love of Christ, and it was first embodied in a leader who could make it visible for the group. Roger Schutz and Steve Moon each had the power to dream and articulate that vision so that others could share it. They first loved, and it was their love that drew first a few then increasing numbers to recognize the loving community with which they wished to be united. We have seen some evidences of how these communities move toward works of justice, and it remains to be shown how the peace which follows must be practiced in freedom.

For your reflection:

How would you feel about being a member of a community like the House of Daybreak? What would be the most difficult adjustment for you?

Questions for Reflection and Discussion

1. Reflect on the various communities to which you belong — on their membership, their goals, and the bond uniting the members. Which communities are most important in your life? Which one has exerted the greatest influence?
2. What part has a community which shares memories of the past or hopes for the future played in your life?
3. Compare the early Christian community described by Luke to the parish community today. What can you do to make your parish a more Christian community reflecting the values of the apostolic community?
4. Show from your own experiences the importance of open communication in relationships and community living.
5. Do you feel that the challenges of the young people in "Second Letter to the People of God" are realistic? What would happen if a significant number of people accepted these challenges? Are you willing to accept them?
6. How would you feel about being a member of a community like the House of Daybreak? What would be the most difficult adjustment for you?
7. If you are not a member of a community working for justice, are you willing to join such a community? What help do you need from this group?

Reading V
PEACE: PRACTICED IN FREEDOM

Section 1

**You will know the truth,
and the truth will set you free.**

John 8:32

We have seen that the process of finding peace begins with the individual setting out upon the search for truth. Each must search for the truth of living more humanly and must realize, to some extent, a harmony between what is seen within self and the ideal that becomes illuminated in the search. The individual then recognizes that others, too, should have this opportunity of experiencing some harmony in their lives and comes to see, as well, that he or she will be stunted in growth toward peace unless they assist others in their search. We have seen that this assistance of others expresses itself in works of justice. The frustrations and disappointments experienced in struggling against oppressive structures drive the individual to seek the support and encouragement of a loving community.

The diversity and outward characteristics of these communities should not distract us from seeing the changes that take place within their individual members. As one experiences the love and support of other members of the community one's sense of being in harmony with these other persons grows. One begins to be aware of greater peace within self and, at the same time, becomes conscious of new strength to use talents and insights to help others to discover the peace growing within them. In spite of this greater inner peace, however, the individual feels that something is missing. One feels that there are obstacles that prevent an even deeper experience of peace and that block efforts at helping others find peace. These obstacles are best described as areas of unfreedom, which often do not yield to our most earnest efforts to eradicate them. How, then, will the individual achieve greater freedom in order to better express peace?

Roger and Steve became freer in their response to the call of God in their life situations because of the loving communities of which they are members. Because the love existing in the community is a sharing in the love of Christ the resulting freedom must somehow be a participation in the freedom of Christ. By reflecting on the freedom of Jesus we can come to appreciate the gift of human freedom and understand the implications of Pope John's phrase that "peace must be practiced in freedom."

If one honestly examines one's own heart, one will discover that there is a darkness, a resistance which speaks of some lack of harmony in one's relationship with God. This is not to say that harmony with God can only be sought after one realizes some peace with self and others. Although we have discussed these processes in a certain sequence, a person's relating to reality cannot be compartmentalized as though different aspects of it can be developed one at a time. Growth in one's relationship with self, others, and God, if it is to be authentic growth, must all go on simultaneously. Each area of growth influences the others, and each depends on progress in the other areas to prevent atrophy of the whole person. There are, however, some aspects of this growth that may be considered more basic than others. Achieving harmony with God is the most delicate aspect of the process since it involves the innermost self, and it is the most directly dependent on the action of the Spirit and the willingness of the person to be healed of all self-centeredness.

In the search for the truth of one's own humanity and in one's cooperation with others in loving community there is a certain initiative on the part of the individual. One feels one is doing something — searching, working for justice, loving and being loved by others. In some ways, the person may feel that growth in inner peace is the reward of this striving. The individual also begins to see that this activity is having an influence on others and thus contributing, in at least a small way, to the peace of the world.

In growing in one's relationship with God the individual may feel, at first, that growth will be the product of her or his own initiative and effort. But there will come a time in the growth process when the individual must face the fact that she or he can do nothing. Faced with this sense of nothingness, the individual can only cry out to Jesus as Peter did in the storm, "Lord, save me" (Matthew 14:30). This cry for help is not so much a plea to be given the power to walk on the water but a plea to be freed from all those incumbrances that are pulling us down into the depths. It can be interpreted as a heartfelt begging, "Jesus, free me." There is still some initiative, some activity required of the individual, but, as we shall see, this effort consists primarily in attempting to be open to the activity of the Spirit.

The essence of Jesus' freedom lay in the love he had for the Father. He was united to the Father's will in all things. This was the perfect expression of freedom because it meant that Jesus in no way was enslaved by outside pressures, by human respect, by any weakness or ignorance within himself, nor any desires contrary to the will of his Father. The love Jesus had for the Father resulted in the perfect freedom in which he lived. He did not find it necessary to speak of freedom often because his whole life was an expression of what it means to be truly free.

The temptations of Jesus in the desert reveal, in a very special way, the extent of Jesus' freedom. At his Baptism the Father had shown, by sign and word, his approval of his Son. Almost as soon as Jesus heard the words of approbation he felt the Spirit drawing him into the desert. Free from any self-seeking, from any desire to take advantage of his favored place in the Father's eyes, Jesus responded to the Spirit and departed to the desert to pray, fast, and listen to the Spirit.

The temptations were specific challenges to the freedom of Jesus. The suggestion to turn stones into bread was an appeal to use power for himself, to put his security in material things. Jesus showed by his response that he was free of the grasp material things can have on human beings. He would use the things of this world only as they expressed his love for the Father.

The second temptation to throw himself from the roof of the temple appealed to the dramatic side of his humanity. What an impressive way to convince the people to listen to his message! Jesus was free from his own ideas of his mission and was able to resist taking things into his own hands. Instead, he waited for the clarification of his mission from the Father; and, as each step became clearer to him, he responded in love.

The third temptation was perhaps the most insidious. The devil took Jesus to a high mountain and promised him all the kingdoms of the world if he would adore him. This was the most attractive temptation because it promised the fulfillment of Jesus' mission immediately. Jesus had come to establish the reign of God, and here was an opportunity to carry out that mission with an ease and completeness beyond his fondest dreams. In rejecting the temptations Jesus surrendered in love to the Father and accepted the Father's plan for his life. This acceptance was not a once-for-all submission but needed to be lived out step by step, day by day. We know that even as his life drew to an end Jesus was still faced with the question, "Are you free enough in my love to accept a cruel death for others?" The struggle was very real; but Jesus could, from his perfect freedom motivated by love of the Father, respond, "Father . . . not my will but yours be done" (Luke 22:42).

If we are to be truly free, we need first of all to be united in love with Jesus. This union of hearts takes place when the individual experiences love in a community and is called to respond in love to others. This is an unselfish love and as such is a participation in the love with which Jesus loved the Father. Sharing in Jesus' love, one shares in his Spirit, and he or she must be willing to be changed by the action of the Spirit. This is not an easy process by any means, but it is necessary if the individual is to be freed from self-

centeredness. This one term is used to include all the enslavements to which we cling so tenaciously. Our blindness is so
deep that we are not even able to perceive with any clarity all the
subtle, and not so subtle, ways in which we cater to our ego.

Some areas of enslavement become obvious with a little reflection and insight. These are the conscious ways we have of
clinging to and grasping material possessions, our own opinion,
reputation, status, and power. These enslavements, because they
are conscious, are usually more readily accessible to the action of
the Spirit. We come to recognize the harm we are doing to ourselves and others by resisting healing in these areas. If we are
sincere in wanting to be free, recognizing and admitting the evil is
the first step toward greater freedom.

Far more difficult to get at are the unconscious enslavements in
our lives. They are not within range of our awareness and, therefore, cannot be brought to the Spirit for healing by our deliberate
action. Even being willing to have these areas of unfreedom revealed to us takes some courage. The revelation is always painful,
for it confronts us with an image of ourselves that is so hard to look
at that we have buried it in the unconscious. We can do nothing to
bring about this revelation except to be willing to cooperate with it
when it does occur. Often the revelation comes in a way that is
totally unexpected and surprising. By accepting the light the Spirit
gives us we open ourselves to the healing power of the same Spirit.
The healing may be a slow process; but one thing we can count on
— through it we will come to share more deeply in the freedom of
Jesus. The more liberated we become, the more we will resemble
Jesus. This increasing resemblance is experienced as a growth in
inner peace, for there is now greater harmony between our lives
and ideal human life as personified by Jesus. We sense a new
harmony in our relationship with the Father as we are able to
address him more sincerely with Jesus, "Abba, Father."

On the night before he died, Jesus promised his disciples that he
would gift them with his peace. He said, "Peace is my farewell to
you, my peace is my gift to you; I do not give it to you as the world
gives peace" (John 14:27). It was after Jesus' most perfect expres-

sion of his love for the Father, when he showed most fully the freedom of his life, that he appeared to his disciples and kept his promise. He greeted them with, "Peace be with you" (John 20:19). He could offer them his peace because they now understood that they were to share in his love for the Father which would give them greater freedom and peace. Sharing Jesus' peace, they needed only to share more fully in his Spirit in order to go out and teach others the way to peace. They were freed on Pentecost from the fears and doubts that still lingered in their hearts and were freed for the work of the Kingdom.

For your reflection:

Have you ever felt completely helpless? How did you react to this experience of your own frailty?

Section 2

One God and Father of all, who is over all, and works through all, and is in all.

Ephesians 4:6

One aspect of Jesus' freedom that needs to be emphasized today is his freedom from any narrowness of vision or parochialism. Jesus came to save everyone, a lesson the early Church had to learn gradually. We know from Acts how difficult it was for the apostles to accept the fact that the Good News was not to be restricted to the Jewish people. It took a vision to convince Peter that the Gentiles were to be admitted to Baptism without first accepting Judaism. After two thousand years of Christianity, can we say that we really believe and live the fact that we are all sisters and brothers, that we are all children of one Father and, therefore, belong to one family?

An honest assessment of our attitude today shows that we are still far from having the global vision that follows from such a faith. There are indications that we are moving in that direction; but before we can have an authentic vision of the world as one we must somehow be freed from our "security straitjacket" — the American frame of mind described so well by Pat and Gerald Mische. We have become so concerned about our own security that at least six governmental departments are focused on some aspect of it. The effect of this national security fixation is to so concentrate on this one human need that all other needs are neglected. Since security is just one of the basic human needs this means that, while more and more material and human resources are being poured into security efforts, the values implied in deeper human living are being bypassed.

Given the "mind set" of our country, the essential question becomes, "How can we break out of this security straitjacket and exercise the freedom we claim we have?" It necessitates a prior change in perspective, a shift of emphasis. Cardinal Roy mentions in his "Reflections on *Pacem in Terris*" a right that we must avail ourselves of today, the right to a vision of the world. In a positive sense, he is saying that an individual has the right to see the world in a unified sense. Each of us has the right to transcend excessive, narrow, state and nationalistic loyalties and to recognize a higher loyalty to the world community. Pope John in *Pacem in Terris* expressed this same concept when he enunciated the right to emigrate, a right which he based on one's membership in the human family. Being a citizen of a particular state does not deprive a person of citizenship in the world community.

At the present time it seems that for the majority of people any thought of world citizenship is out of the question or, at best, very unimportant. Yet, if a complete destruction of the world and annihilation of the human race is to be avoided, the new type of freedom implied by it must grow and expand throughout the world. Individuals must become free of the narrowness that fails to see the interconnectedness of the whole human family.

There is an ever-increasing awareness among thinking people today of our economic dependence. The oil crisis of 1973 was a real blessing for the United States. For the first time in the lives of many people we were made to feel our dependence on other nations. We are almost always in a position of control, so that our inability to get the oil we needed was a salutary shock. Unfortunately, in large measure, the lesson learned was soon forgotten when our needs were again being met. Instead of making us acknowledge our dependence and accept our interconnectedness, the motivational thrust of the lesson was turned to renewing our efforts to make the United States independent in its energy requirements in the future. We missed the opportunity of leading the world to a greater consciousness that we are one family.

The fantastic growth in population over the past twenty years has had the effect of drawing people closer in a physical way. It is no longer possible for many people to isolate themselves from other human beings. In large cities the very density of population is forcing people to look for better ways of living in peace and harmony. Many problems — such as alcoholism, wife and child abuse, drug addiction, and the disintegration of family life — if not rooted in overcrowding are at least aggravated by the lack of privacy and space to be alone. This partly explains the popularity of transcendental meditation and other forms of going within one's self to the inner center of quiet. Given the trend to greater interdependence recognized as taking place in today's world, a more realistic approach would seem to be learning to live in greater closeness rather than trying to escape the situation. How this is to be done would require a book in itself, but it seems safe to say that one of the essential prerequisites would be an increase in the ability of more and more people to find inner peace.

The first release of atomic energy in Arizona revealed promising spiritual possibilities in addition to the more immediately evident and terrifying physical possibilities. This momentous event had been accomplished in a relatively short period of time (about three years) because hundreds of people had used their brains on this single project. It showed in a dramatic new way the effect of channeling the energies of a number of exceptional minds into one organized effort.

This was the most profound effect of the atomic blast. It evoked a sense of the possibility of achieving goals beyond the technological improvement of the surface of the earth and beyond the accumulation of external riches. Human beings were becoming free from the struggle to control the forces of nature and would be able to turn their attention to their own growth. They would be able to investigate the possibilities of developing the human potential for greater physical and psychological perfection. Witness already our widespread involvement in physical fitness programs and the explosion of knowledge through the proliferation of computers.

While we must admit that there is a dark side to this picture and that the first atomic blast has left behind it a cloud of fear of impending disaster in the hearts of people all over the world, we must not lose sight of the other side. Scientists from all over the world are collaborating in medical research, space exploration, and agricultural experiments. Teams of technicians from First World countries not only send the results of their technology to developing nations but go themselves to share their skills and knowledge. Instead of forcing our superior technology on poor countries, we are becoming more sensitive to the type of machinery and equipment that will be most useful to them. All these forms of cooperation are capable of bringing about a deeper understanding among peoples and the sympathy that will lead to love and peace.

The people involved in these cooperative efforts are expressing the deeper inner freedom which they have experienced. They have been freed from a biased, narrow vision which sees only the limited confines of their own city, country, or nation as a suitable center for expending their energies. They have a global sense that recognizes that other areas of the world have greater need of their talents and skills, and they have the freedom to go to the members of the human family that need them most.

For your reflection:

Do you see any evidence that nuclear power is uniting the human family?

Section 3

God has given us the wisdom to understand fully the mystery, the plan he was pleased to decree in Christ, to be carried out in the fullness of time: namely, to bring all things in the heavens and on earth into one under Christ's headship.

Ephesians 1:9-10

As we reflect on what is required for individual peace and realize the impact that peaceful people can have on the peace of the world, we begin to see similarities between struggling for justice and working to establish the Kingdom of God. These similarities might lead us to question if working for justice and efforts to advance the Kingdom are identical. We might be tempted to answer in the affirmative in light of the statement that "action on behalf of justice seems to us a constitutive element of the Gospel" (Synod of Bishops, *Justice in the World*). If we understand working for justice in terms of providing those conditions in which human beings can reach their potential and if we consider the fulfillment of the Kingdom as the endpoint of salvation, the question becomes, "What is the relationship between human development and salvation?" Looking at the question from an even broader perspective, we see that it involves a basic understanding of human history and salvation.

In reflecting on this basic problem in the light of the Old Testament, one thinks immediately of the Exodus event. In the history of the Jewish people this event holds a unique place. There were other times when they were released from captivity, from Babylon and Assyria for example, but the departure from Egypt and the subsequent wandering in the desert had unparalleled effects on the self-understanding of the Israelites. They understood, perhaps for the first time, that it was God who was their liberator, that they were dependent on him for their very sustenance. They learned that in a special way God was teaching them his ways. He was setting them apart for a special relationship with him. We could say that the whole desert experience was one of arriving at a sense of identity, a time of realization of their dignity as a people loved by God and their responsibility to fidelity.

As we read the Exodus account in Scripture, we could consider it and treat it as part of human history, the liberation of a people held in slavery. But it is also clear that this very same segment of human history, on a deeper level, is also part of salvation history, that is, it is also a part of the account of *God's dealing with humankind.* The writer of Exodus in no way implies that this is *merely* human history. The continued action of God — from the birth of Moses, his preparation for his leadership role, through all the attempts at escape from Egypt — shines through the human struggle. In the desert, God is continually instructing, by word and deed, the people he has covenanted with on Sinai.

That the Jews were aware of the other dimensions of this event is evident from their annual celebration of Passover. They do not recall the saving action of God as something which took place in the past and is completed. Their Passover celebration brings the event into the present so that once again they are inserted into the action in a very real way. The saving action of God in the Exodus continues to be God's salvific care of his chosen ones.

More than that, the Exodus is repeated and its salvific power released in the life of each person who is willing to be inserted into the mystery of God's ongoing redemptive activity. The inner liberation from the slavery of self-centeredness in its cyclic repetition results in an ever-deepening experience of being grasped and bonded to God.

Looking only at the Exodus and its prolongation in human history, one might very well conclude that human history and salvation history coincide, in the sense that God's activity enters into human life so intimately. If, however, we try to distinguish aspects of history as to their source, the perspective changes.

If we consider human history as those events flowing from the action of human beings and salvation history as specifically God's activity, incidents in the Old Testament that expressed the infidelity of human beings to God would seem outside salvation history, in that the evil involved could not be seen as God's action. A further clue is found in the prophets. The repentance and the works of justice the prophets called for are both dependent upon the initiative of God. Both required some response from individuals, but, primarily, it was God who was to reconcile and to liberate. In the books of Amos, Isaiah, Jeremiah, Micah, and Hosea, the change called for in society is seen as possible only if there is first a change of heart; and it is God who provides for the welfare of human beings while, at the same time, calling for their response.

In its study of this question, the International Theological Commission issues a special warning about taking the social dimension of the New Testament in an authentic sense. The Father's love in sending his Son to establish the Kingdom takes priority over any concern for relationships on the human level. The belief that the Kingdom was at hand eclipsed the urgency of providing for human needs. We find evidence of this attitude in Paul's insistence that Christians should work and not be content waiting for the Second Coming of Jesus. He goes so far as to say that those who do not work should not eat.

The Theological Commission summarized its study on human development and salvation in the New Testament by stating:

In the light of the New Testament, society is not genuinely changed unless men and women are reconciled with God and with one another. Only if men and women become a new creation by conversion and justice can the style of human living be adequately and steadily improved.

Gaudium et Spes points out that the ordinary activities of men and women in providing the necessities of life for themselves and their families "unfolds the Creator's work and contributes to the realization in history of the divine plan." The development that takes place *in the person* through this human activity is of more value than any material, external wealth. Human activity, however, is always in danger of being subjected to selfishness, destroying its ability to bring about true unity. This unfortunate situation can be overcome by immersing human activity in the Paschal Mystery. Christ is at work through the energy of his Spirit, inspiring and strengthening individuals to become more human and move the earth closer to its goal. After having established the close link between human activity for human development and the good of all society with the saving action of God in the world, *Gaudium et Spes* maintains that human development and the growth of Christ's Kingdom are not identical. The linkage between the two must not be allowed to cloud the fact that they are different.

Because this question is so relevant the International Theological Commission studied the question and published its conclusions in October 1976. The Commission made it clear that the conclusions are not definitive but that they are based on the current status of theological research. In the final report, translated by Reverend Walter J. Burghardt, S.J., the results of the study are stated in two principles:

1. On the one hand, existential history is in a way the locus where the world is so deeply transformed that it reaches as far as the mystery of God; and that is why love and its fruits abide. It is ultimately for this reason that there can be a link between salvation and human welfare, between salvation and human rights. But they are not linked to perfection because the eschatological fulfillment "takes away" existential history.

2. On the other hand, the kingdom of God directs history and utterly transcends all the possibilities of earthly fulfillment; it presents itself, therefore, as the action of God. This involves a certain break with that world, no matter what perfection we recognize therein. This discontinuity in our individual stories we experience as death, but the same discontinuity precisely as "transformation" touches the whole of history; it is the world's "destruction."

What does all this say to the individual who in loving community strives to change conditions in the contemporary world toward greater equality and freedom for all people? Once the basic principle is established that divine worship, prayer, the Eucharist, and other sacraments must take first place in one's priorities, then one can say that all loving service of one's neighbor, all one's attempts to change unjust structures, are contributing to the progress of humanity and are also helping in the furtherance of the Kingdom. It must be remembered, however, that one's most earnest efforts for justice may apparently fail but that these same efforts, in God's providence, may be successful, looked at from within the Kingdom. Nothing that one does for God or neighbor is ever wasted in the mystery of God's economy of salvation. The justice advocate must also admit that the Kingdom is already present within the hearts of men and women and yet, when human justice triumphs in peace, completion of the Kingdom may still be to come. It is only when all things are brought to Christ that the search for truth finds its goal. Then justice will triumph in the unification of love and all will be brought to the peace and freedom of the Kingdom fulfilled.

For your reflection:

Show how working for the spread of the Kingdom can involve the individual in works of justice. Is this always necessarily so? Give some examples to support your answers.

Questions for Reflection and Discussion

1. Have you ever felt completely helpless? How did you react to this experience of your own frailty?
2. Do you experience your own freedom when you do God's will as Jesus did?
3. Are there any parallels to Jesus' temptations in your life?
4. As you reflect on your life, what areas of unfreedom do you find?
5. How do you feel about being challenged to escape from the "security straitjacket"? What do your feelings tell you about your vision of the world?
6. What responsibilities follow from the fact that you are a citizen of the world community?
7. Do you see any evidence that nuclear power is uniting the human family?
8. Show how working for the spread of the Kingdom can involve the individual in works of justice. Is this always necessarily so? Give some examples to support your answer.

SUGGESTED READING

Camara, Helder, Dom. *Revolution through Peace.* New York: Harper and Row Publishers, 1971.

Cassidy, Sheila. *Audacity to Believe.* Cleveland, Ohio: William Collins and World Publishing Co. Inc., 1977.

Douglas, James W. *The Non-Violent Cross.* New York: Macmillan Company, 1966.

Gandhi, M. K. *The Story of My Experiments with Truth.* Washington, D.C.: Public Affairs Press, 1948.

Gremillion, Joseph, ed. *The Gospel of Peace and Justice.* New York: Orbis Books, 1976.

Gutierrez, Gustavo. *A Theology of Liberation.* Maryknoll: Orbis Books, 1973.

Haughey, John C., ed. *The Faith That Does Justice.* New York: Paulist Press, 1977.

Kripalani, Krishna. *Gandhi: A Life.* Mystic, Connecticut: Verry Inc., 1968.

Merton, Thomas. *Faith and Violence.* Notre Dame, Indiana: University of Notre Dame Press, 1968.

_____. *The Nonviolent Alternative.* New York: Farrar, Straus & Giroux, Inc., 1971, 1980.

Mishe, Gerald and Mishe, Patricia. *Toward a Human World Order.* New York: Paulist Press, 1977.

Petrement, Simone. *Simone Weil.* New York: Pantheon Books, 1976.

Ruether, Rosemary Radford. *Liberation Theology.* New York: Paulist Press, 1972.

Shea, John. *What a Modern Catholic Believes about Sin.* Chicago: The Thomas More Press, 1971.

U.S. Catholic Bishops' pastoral letter on peace and war, *The Challenge of Peace: God's Promise and Our Response* and the official Summary of the pastoral letter. United States Catholic Conference, 1983.